Critical Thinking with Algorithms

Student Workbook

First Edition

Version 1.0

2

Critical Thinking with Algorithms: Student Workbook
First Edition
Version 1.0

Published by
1423 Interests LLC
Houston, Texas USA

www.CriticalThinkingWithAlgorithms.com

ISBN 978-0-57-872635-9

© 2020   Mark Spencer Palmer

Cover design by Matthew Reynolds

All rights reserved. No part of this book may be reproduced in any form by any means without written permission of the publisher.

TABLE OF CONTENTS

INTRODUCTION
ABOUT THIS WORKBOOK

This workbook and the accompanying videos will equip students to think critically, create solutions, find answers to challenging questions, solve problems, and make decisions....using algorithms.

Questions about using this workbook

Is anything else needed to use this workbook?
Yes, you will need access to the accompanying video for each chapter. Each video is approximately 15 minutes in length and introduces and explains the concepts in each chapter. Students should view each chapter's video before they work on the Review Questions and Investigation. If you do not already have access to the videos, please visit the following page to request access:

`https://www.CriticalThinkingWithAlgorithms.com/video`

or use this QR code to access the link:

Does this course require computer programming?
This is not a programming course. This is a conceptual introduction to critical thinking with algorithms. However, in Chapter 7 (Draw), students do create a script using "turtle graphics" in the Python programming language to complete the Investigation. This is a simplified version of traditional Python programming.

What ages or grades should take this course?
This workbook is designed for high school students (Grades 9 through 12) as an introduction to procedural, critical thinking and some computer science topics. But this workbook can also be appropriate for advanced middle school students or adults who wish to learn more about algorithms. Although Algebra 1 is not a strict prerequisite for this course, many topics in this workbook require critical thinking at a level similar to solving an algebra problem.

Is this course intended only for Science, Math, or pre-engineering students?
No, all students can benefit from this course. Although several of the chapter topics are related to computer science concepts, this workbook is designed to be used by a wide range of students. Students will be exposed to algorithms spanning a variety of subjects and techniques, including creative writing and brainstorming.

What students will learn in this course?
Students will learn how to do the following:
1. Apply algorithmic thinking to solve everyday problems in daily life. Students can develop "how-to guides" for topics that directly benefit them, such as the following:
- Learning: how to study for a test, how to teach a new concept
- Business: how to streamline a business process
- Project management: how to decompose a large project into smaller tasks
- Problem solving: how to improve a process that I am dissatisfied with, how to find the root cause of a problem, how to decompose a complex problem into simpler, component parts.

2. Understand fundamental computer science concepts (e.g., sorting, searching, arrays, recursion, boolean logic), without needing to learn the exact syntax of a programming language. Instead, we will focus on the underlying concepts and principles. A student can pursue computer programming, if interested, using this course as a conceptual foundation.

3. Follow detailed written instructions. Students learn to complete detailed lessons that involve following existing algorithms and creating new algorithms.

4. Create instructions and explanations for helping others, completing a task, or preserving knowledge. Students learn to express themselves using both of the following:
- mathematical principles and language, using logic and precision
- linguistic principles, using unambiguous English sentences

5. Evaluate the succinctness and precision of prose. Most of the algorithms in this course are written in English, not computer code. Students must write with clarity since their instructions will be evaluated by others' ability to follow their instructions.

6. Improve poor processes and algorithms. Students can identify what needs to change in an existing process to achieve a better result. Students learn how to be "a part of the solution, not just part of the problem."

How can this workbook be used as part of a curriculum?
- **STEM students** can use this workbook as a foundational course prior to learning formal programming. Topics in this workbook may provide inspiration for developing apps or for finding new solutions to problems.
- **Younger students** can skip sections, questions, or chapters that are too abstract or difficult to master.
- **Classically-educated students** can take this course after a course in formal logic. This creates a pair of courses that complement each other.
- **Students working in teams** can complete the Investigations in small groups. Students can creatively solve problems and explore real-world algorithms using hands-on investigations. Small groups can explore the discussion questions.
- **Homeschool students** can complete the Investigations individually without the need for additional lectures or instruction. The Investigations, Review Questions, and Discussion Questions can be completed at home. Homeschool students can also work with other students to complete each chapter in a co-op or collaborative setting.
- **Advanced students** who enjoy the concepts can use the chapter topic as a launching point for more in-depth work, such as the following:
  - apply the same concepts to a deeper investigation or project
  - develop an independent project to create a new algorithm or refine an existing algorithm
  - create models or simulations that demonstrate their understanding of the chapter's topic

- explore the discussion questions in more depth
- conduct separate research into types of algorithms related to the chapter topic
- create computer programs that work to support the investigation or chapter objectives

How can an instructor create a course using this workbook?

This course can be taught in one semester by covering one chapter per week. Or it can be taught in two semesters by covering one chapter every two weeks. The following activities can be combined to create one-week or two-week lesson plans for each chapter.

Core Student Activities

- Students watch the video for each chapter and take notes using the Notes section of this workbook.
- Students write answers to Review Questions in this workbook.
- Students complete the chapter Investigation.
  - The Investigations can be worked on individually, or in pairs or in small groups.
- Students share Investigation results with the rest of the group.

Additional Student Activities

- Students answer the Discussion Questions individually as preparation for group discussion.
- Students work in pairs or groups to answer the Discussion Questions.
- Students present answers to the Discussion Questions and engage in a larger group discussion.
- Students prepare a summary or presentation that provides a chapter overview and incorporates the chapter's objectives.

Group activities (led by an instructor or group leader)

- Ask a student to introduce and describe each chapter's topic from notes or memory.
- Conduct interactive exercises or question-and-answer related to the Investigation.
- Prepare students for the upcoming Investigation topic by providing suggestions and guidance.
- Discuss the chapter's topic by asking open-ended questions such as "Why is this topic relevant?"
- Work as a large group (or in small groups) to solve a short problem related to the chapter topic (e.g., understand the causes of an accident, decipher a message written on the board)
- Provide supplemental detail about the week's topic. This could include the following:
  - Recap concepts from the video
  - Tell stories or provide examples from personal experience
  - Give examples of the concept applied to real-world situations
- Answer student questions.
- Provide a demonstration of the week's topic.

How is each lesson structured?

Each week's lesson has a verb for its title. The verb (e.g., "Hide") serves as the topic for the lesson and describes one way that algorithms can be used. This one-word focus makes the purpose of the lesson clear and keeps the course action-oriented.

Each chapter includes an assignment called an "Investigation." This is a case-study, a problem, or a collection of exercises that the students can use critical thinking to solve.

Can this course be taught online or using the flipped classroom?
Yes. The students can work independently to view the videos, answer the review questions, and complete the Investigation. Then students can meet to discuss, interact, and review the material together.

Who is qualified to teach this?
In a school setting, the chapters in this workbook can be taught by a math or science instructor.
In a homeschool setting, a motivated parent or student can work through all the questions and Investigations.
This text explores a variety of engaging topics (e.g., steganography, cryptography, sorting, estimation) at an introductory level so that there is no need for specialized course preparation or computer programming.

CHAPTER 1
IDENTIFY

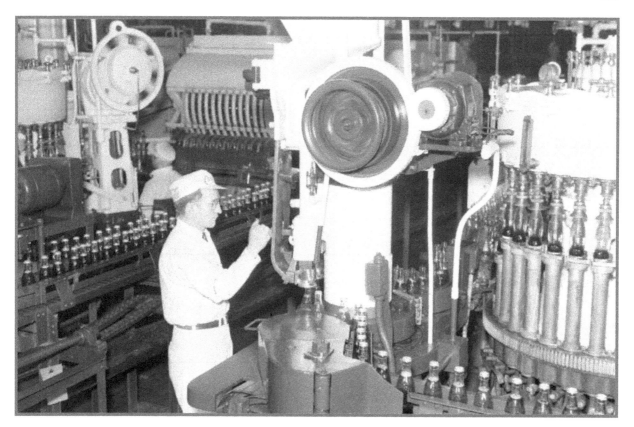

Employees working in a Coca-Cola bottling plant in 1941. The recipe for Coca Cola is an example of a private, highly formal algorithm. A recipe like this may also be called a "secret formula."

KEY QUESTION

How can I identify an algorithm?

OBJECTIVES

After completing this chapter, students should be able to do the following:
1. List and describe different types of algorithms.
2. Explain why algorithms are useful.
3. Define, in your own words, the *black box model*.
4. Explain why the *IAO model* is used in this course instead of the black box model.
5. Describe the types of languages that can be used to create algorithms.
6. Write a short summary of the chapter, answering the key question.

REVIEW QUESTIONS

Answer these questions with the help of the video:

1. What is an algorithm?

_____

_____

2. What are some synonyms for "algorithm?"

_____

_____

3. What are some things algorithms do for us?

_____

_____

4. What are different types of algorithms? Provide examples.

_____

_____

_____

_____

5. Why are algorithms useful?

_____

_____

_____

6. What languages can be used to write algorithms?

_____

_____

7. Fill out the chart below by adding one of your own examples to each quadrant:

Private		
Visibility		
Public		
	Informal	Formal

Formality

8. Label the following diagram according to the IAO model:

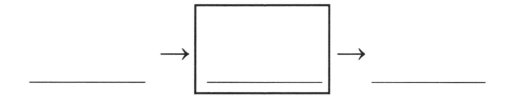

NOTES

_____

_____

_____

_____

_____

_____

_____

_____

_____

_____

_____

_____

_____

_____

_____

_____

DISCUSSION QUESTIONS

1. What types of algorithms do you interact with? What useful things do these algorithms do?
2. What algorithms do you use most often?
3. How would you improve the algorithms that you use regularly?
4. Have you created algorithms? If so, what types?
5. What are some examples of valuable algorithms? What makes them so valuable? Where would you place them on the Formality vs. Visibility grid?

INVESTIGATION

You will be identifying algorithms in different real-world scenarios. For each of the photos below, list several algorithms that are used by people, machines, or computers. It may help to consider the following for each photo:

- What information do people working in each scenario need access to?
- What machines are used? Do these machines have built-in algorithms?
- What computers are used? What tasks are the computers performing? What algorithms are needed?
- What kind of things are being done or created? What algorithms are needed for that?

Scenario 1: A Grocery Store

This person, machine, or computer...	Uses an algorithm to do this...
the cash register	calculate the total amount of the customer's purchase, including tax

Scenario 2: An airplane cockpit

This person, machine, or computer…	Uses an algorithm to do this…

Scenario 3: An artist's studio

This person, machine, or computer…	Uses an algorithm to do this…

Scenario 4: A farm with a barn, silos, and wind turbines

This person, machine, or computer…	Uses an algorithm to do this…

Scenario 5: A container ship traveling through the Panama Canal

This person, machine, or computer...	Uses an algorithm to do this...

CHAPTER 2
HIDE

A United States one hundred dollar bill. Each bill contains watermarks and hidden features that help distinguish genuine bills from counterfeit ones.

KEY QUESTION

How can I design an algorithm to hide a message?

OBJECTIVES

After completing this chapter, students should be able to do the following:

1. Define *steganography*.
2. Explain the purpose of steganography.
3. Define and describe: *cover medium, data to hide, stego algorithm, stego key,* and *stego medium*.
4. Write a short summary of the chapter, answering the key question.

REVIEW QUESTIONS

Answer these questions with the help of the video:

1. What is the etymology of the word steganography? Do dinosaurs have anything to do with this?

_____

_____

_____

2. What are some examples of steganography?

_____

_____

3. How have you seen steganography used in your personal life? Elaborate in 2-3 sentences.

_____

_____

_____

_____

_____

_____

NOTES

_____

_____

_____

_____

_____

_____

_____

_____

_____

_____

_____

_____

_____

_____

_____

_____

DISCUSSION QUESTIONS

1. How could you begin to tell if a digital image had a hidden message?
2. Is "copy protection" (which prevents someone from copying a digital file) a form of steganography? Why or why not?
3. How long of a message could you hide in a color photo on your phone? How would you hide the message?
4. If you were shipping someone a suitcase, what are some ways to deliver a hidden message?
5. If you were on a phone call, what are some ways that you could deliver a hidden message?

INVESTIGATION

You will be designing an algorithm to create a steganogram, which is a hidden message. The **input** will be a message of your choice. The **algorithm** will be the method that you use to hide the message. The **output** will be your hidden message.

1. Write your "data to hide":
This is an eight to fifteen letter message of your choice

---

2. Choose a "cover medium."
This is how you will hide your message. This could be an image, text, drawing, object, or anything that obscures or disguises your message. Use your imagination! This can be something that you create or something that you already have, as long as it doesn't require any special equipment or chemicals (this probably rules out invisible ink and microdots).

3. Create your "stego medium" (also called "steganogram")
This step creates your "steganogram" by combining your "data to hide" and your "cover medium." If someone looks at your steganogram, they should see something that does NOT look like a hidden message. But if someone knows how to look for your message, they should be able to find your message.

4. On the next page, write down your "stego algorithm."
This is the guide to allow someone to find the hidden message. It is the written key that will unlock your hidden message and reveal your "data to hide."

Your stego algorithm should have numbered steps like a recipe that someone else could follow, for example:
1. First do this
2. then do this
3. then do this

There is not a minimum or maximum number of steps, as long as your algorithm is understandable by someone else who reads it.

You may wish to test your steganogram by first seeing if someone can find your "**data to hide**" by simply looking at your **steganogram** (Hopefully, they will not find your hidden message quickly!). Then give your "stego algorithm" to this same person and see if they can follow the instructions (without you helping them) and find your "data to hide."

My Stego Algorithm

_____

_____

_____

_____

_____

_____

_____

_____

_____

_____

_____

_____

_____

_____

_____

_____

_____

_____

_____

_____

_____

24

CHAPTER 3
ESTIMATE

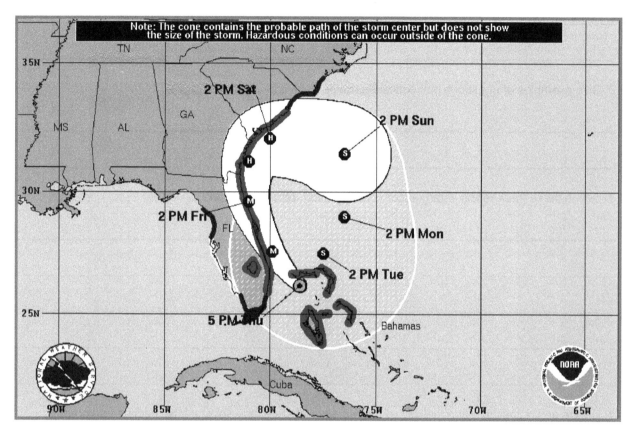

Forecasted path of Hurricane Matthew (2016), a Category 5 storm that never made landfall along the Florida coast. Storm tracks like these are good examples of estimation algorithms.

KEY QUESTION
How can I estimate something using an algorithm?

OBJECTIVES
After completing this chapter, students should be able to do the following:
1. Explain why we need estimates.
2. Explain seven estimation techniques: *Decomposing*, *Modeling*, *Trend Following*, *Interpolation*, *Extrapolation*, *Correlation*, and *Sampling*.
3. Identify which estimation technique is in use for a given estimation algorithm.
4. List some common estimation algorithms that we interact with in our everyday lives.
5. Develop an estimation algorithm to solve a particular problem.
6. Write a short summary of the chapter, answering the key question.

REVIEW QUESTIONS

Answer these questions with the help of the video:

1. Why is estimation useful?

_____

_____

_____

2. Give examples of questions that estimation helps answer.

_____

_____

3. Define these three terms: interpolation, extrapolation, and correlation.

_____

_____

_____

_____

_____

4. Create an original question that would require several steps and several intermediate estimates to arrive at the final estimate. Some sample patterns are as follows:
- What is the number of _____ in _____?
- How many _____ are consumed by _____?
- What is the total amount of _____ in _____?

This type of question is called a Fermi problem, named after physicist Enrico Fermi who was known for his ability to make quick, reasonable approximations.

_____

_____

_____

_____

NOTES

_____

_____

_____

_____

_____

_____

_____

_____

_____

_____

_____

_____

_____

_____

DISCUSSION QUESTIONS

1. What algorithm could you develop for solving Fermi problems? How well does your algorithm work when trying to solve the following Fermi problems?
   - How many baseballs are used during all Major League games in one season?
   - How many mobile phones are there in the world?
   - How many rivets are there in a Boeing 737 jet airplane?

2. What are some new Fermi problems that would be interesting to solve? What could make your Fermi problem easier? or more difficult?

3. How could the output of an algorithm be used to refine the algorithm itself? Provide some examples of this.

INVESTIGATION

You will be designing an estimation algorithm to guess the number of beans in a jar.

Setting up this Investigation (for the instructor or group leader)
This Investigation requires a few items to be prepared beforehand. These items can be done by the instructor or by each group that is completing this Investigation.

a. Find a small, clear jar and fill it with dried beans or jelly beans. Don't count the beans as you put them in the jar. In the example below, an instant coffee jar has been filled with black beans.

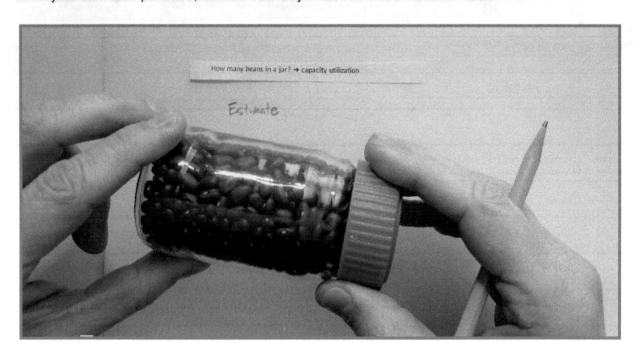

b. Make the jar of beans available to everyone who will be completing this Investigation. Or provide photos or video of the jar filled with beans.

Investigation Instructions for the student

1. Use the IAO model to understand the inputs, algorithm, and outputs for this Investigation.

- The Inputs will be anything that you can observe or measure about the beans, the jar, or any other relevant item. You can also get inputs from other sources, such as something you research online or in a reference book.
- The Algorithm will be the step-by-step process of using the inputs to create the output.
- The Output will be the estimated number of beans in the jar.

2. Design a step-by-step algorithm using your inputs that will result in an output.
Your algorithm should work with a different jar and different beans. Your algorithm should not be so specific that it only works for this particular combination of jar and beans.

3. Write down your algorithm.

Use the space below. Create a step-by-step guide for how to combine, analyze, or use your inputs to create your output. There is no minimum or maximum number of steps, as long as your algorithm is understandable by someone else who reads it.

4. Make an estimate for the number of beans in the jar. Write your estimate here:_____

5. Compare your estimate with other students. What accounts for the variation between the different estimates? Count the beans in the jar and compare your estimate with the actual number of beans. Who was closest? Why? What could make your algorithm better?

You also can fill the jar with a different type of object (e.g., larger beans, marbles, coins, lentils) and see how well your algorithm performs.

My Estimation Algorithm

_____

_____

_____

_____

_____

_____

_____

_____

_____

_____

_____

_____

_____

_____

_____

_____

30

CHAPTER 4
SORT

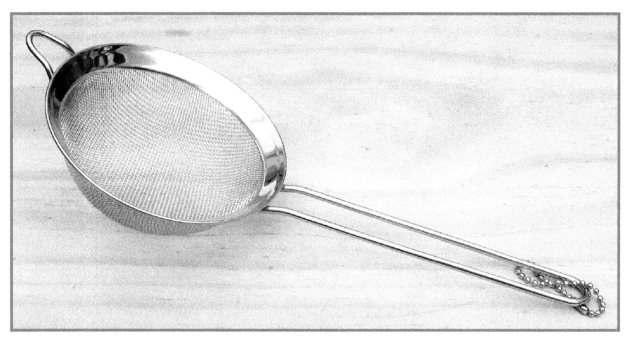

A sieve separates items of different sizes, such as rocks and sand, or pasta and water.
This is an example of sorting.

KEY QUESTION
How can we sort a list of things using an algorithm?

OBJECTIVES
After completing this chapter, students should be able to do the following:
1. Define *array*.
2. Explain the benefits of sorting.
3. Explain the difference between searching and sorting.
4. Explain the purpose of *Big 'O'* notation.
5. List and briefly describe each of the three sorting methods described in this chapter.
6. Write a short summary of the chapter, answering the key question.

REVIEW QUESTIONS

Answer these questions with the help of the video:

1. What determines the complexity of a sorting algorithm? Why is understanding complexity important to computer scientists?

_____

_____

_____

_____

2. What are some sorting algorithms, and what are their major differences?

_____

_____

_____

3. What is Big 'O' Notation and why is it useful?

_____

_____

_____

4. What are things that you need to sort at school or at home? Which sorting methods do you find yourself using the most? Why?

_____

_____

_____

NOTES

_____

_____

_____

_____

_____

_____

_____

_____

_____

_____

_____

_____

_____

_____

_____

_____

_____

DISCUSSION QUESTIONS
1. Why does one need to sort things?
2. In what situations would rapid sorting be needed?
3. What kind of information does the government, your school, a business, or a website collect about you? Provide some examples. How do you think that information is sorted, viewed, and used?
4. What are the most important things in your life to keep sorted?

INVESTIGATION

For this Investigation you will be designing an algorithm to sort 50 slips of paper.

1. Understand the output and inputs of your algorithm.
- The input will be 50 pieces of paper, numbered from 1 to 50.
  - These will be mixed up in a random order.
- The algorithm will be a step-by-step sorting process that you design below.
- The output will be a sorted stack, from 01 on top of the stack to 50 on the bottom.

2. Design a step-by-step algorithm using your input(s) that will result in the desired output.
Your algorithm should be understandable and be able to be followed by someone else who reads it. One person should be able to do it alone. Faster is better.

3. Write your algorithm.
This is the step-by-step guide for what you do to your input(s) to create your output. There is no minimum or maximum number of steps, as long as your algorithm is understandable by someone else who reads it.

_____

_____

_____

_____

_____

_____

_____

_____

_____

_____

_____

_____

4. Time yourself using your algorithm.

You will need the following:
- 50 pieces of paper, numbered 1 to 50. You can cut out the slips at the end of this chapter.
- A clear surface for the sorting to occur, such as a table or the floor.
- A timer or stopwatch or someone to time you.
- Your written sorting algorithm from Step 3.

Thoroughly shuffle the slips of paper and place the unsorted stack in front of you. Once you are ready, start the timer and pick up the stack to begin sorting the cards. When all the slips of paper are sorted from 1 to 50, place the stack back on the table and stop the timer.

5. Record your results

Repeat your sort algorithm three times and record your times in the table below. Calculate your average sort time.

Algorithm Results	Duration (in seconds)
First Sort	
Second Sort	
Third Sort	
Average Sort Time	

6. Have a race

If you are learning this chapter with others, have a sorting contest. Have each student start with their own stack of shuffled slips. The first one to sort their stack wins.

01	11	21	31	41
02	12	22	32	42
03	13	23	33	43
04	14	24	34	44
05	15	25	35	45
06	16	26	36	46
07	17	27	37	47
08	18	28	38	48
09	19	29	39	49
10	20	30	40	50

CHAPTER 5
SOLVE

A self-similar fractal known as a Menger sponge. Fractals are excellent examples of recursion. Each side of the cube is divided into nine squares, with the middle square removed. This process repeats infinitely as the squares get smaller and smaller.

KEY QUESTION
How can I use an algorithm to solve a puzzle?

OBJECTIVES
After completing this chapter, students should be able to do the following:
1. Explain how a *recursive algorithm* works and how it can be helpful.
2. Explain how a *factorial function* works and how it involves recursion.
3. Describe the *Towers of Hanoi* puzzle.
4. Write a short summary of the chapter, answering the key question.

REVIEW QUESTIONS

Answer these questions with the help of the video:

1. What is the etymology of the word *recursive*?

_____

_____

_____

2. What is the difference between recursion and repetition?

_____

_____

_____

_____

3. How can we solve factorials using a recursive algorithm?

_____

_____

_____

_____

_____

NOTES

_____

_____

_____

_____

_____

_____

_____

_____

_____

_____

_____

_____

_____

_____

_____

_____

_____

FOR DISCUSSION
1. What is the purpose of a recursive algorithm?
2. What are some uses for recursive algorithms? What could you solve by using a recursive algorithm?
3. Are recursive algorithms more complex or more straightforward than other algorithms? Why?
4. What are some real-world examples of recursive algorithms?

INVESTIGATION

For this Investigation you will be following a recursive algorithm to solve a puzzle known as the "Towers of Hanoi." This is an old puzzle that involves a set number of disks placed on three separate Pegs. We will use four disks. Here is a side view:

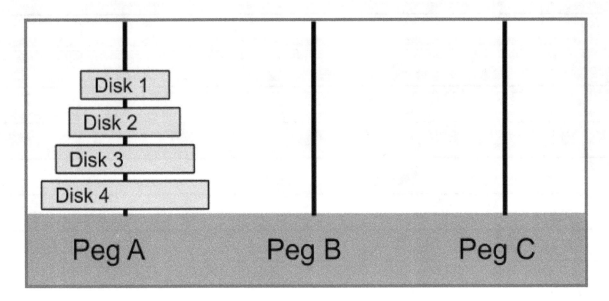

The object of the puzzle is to move all of the disks from Peg A to Peg C, following these rules:
- You can only move one disk at a time.
- You cannot place a larger disk on top of a smaller disk
- After each move, each disk must be on a peg. You may not use the table or space between pegs.

1. Understand the input and output of the puzzle
- The Inputs
  - 3 pegs: Peg A, Peg B, and Peg C. Peg B and Peg C will be empty when you start.
  - 4 disks stacked on Peg A, sorted from largest disk on the bottom to smallest disk on the top.
- The Algorithm will be the process you take to move all the disks from Peg A to Peg C.
- The Output will be a stack of disks on Peg C, identical to the original stack on Peg A.

2. Setup your disks and pegs
If you don't have a wooden version of this puzzle, as shown in the photo, you can use four slips of paper on a page with lines representing three pegs. You may cut out slips of paper at the end of this chapter to use as "disks."

2. Follow the algorithm on the next page to solve the puzzle using four disks (*n* = 4) as the input.
Start with all four the disks on Peg A (the left position). Move all the disks to Peg C while following the rules of the puzzle.

3. Make a list of all the moves required to solve the puzzle using 4 Disks.
Name the Pegs A, B, and C (left to right), and number the disks 1 to 4 (smallest to largest).
When you move a disk to a Peg, write down the number of the disk you moved and the letter of the Peg you moved the disk to (eg: 1B, 2C, 4A, 3B).

_____

_____

_____

_____

_____

_____

How many total moves did it take you to move the four disks from Peg A to Peg C?
Write that number here:

Generalized Algorithm
for moving a stack of disks in the Towers of Hanoi puzzle
(source: hackerearth.com)

For a given N number of disks, the way to accomplish the task in a minimum number of steps is:
    Step 1. Move the top N−1 disks to an intermediate peg.
    Step 2. Move the bottom disk to the destination peg.
    Step 3. Finally, move the N−1 disks from the intermediate peg to the destination peg.

Now let's see how we can use this Generalized Algorithm to solve the Towers of Hanoi puzzle.

For this Investigation we want to move 4 disks to Peg C.
So we can use (N = 4) and (destination peg = Peg C) in the Generalized Algorithm and we get this specific method to solve the puzzle in a minimum number of steps:
    Step 1. Move the top 3 disks to an intermediate peg, which is Peg B.
    Step 2. Move the bottom disk (Disk 4) to the destination peg, which is Peg C.
    Step 3. Finally, move the 3 disks from the intermediate peg (Peg B) to the destination peg (Peg C).

But then how do we move 3 disks, which we need to do in Step 1 and Step 3?

To move 3 disks, we can return again (that is, **recurse**) to the Generalized Algorithm and use N=3 to create a new set of instructions. This new set of instructions for moving 3 disks will then require us to move 2 disks.

To move 2 disks, we can use the Generalized Algorithm yet again to find the easiest method, as follows:
- Move Disk 1 disk to an intermediate peg
- Move Disk 2 to the destination peg
- Finally, move Disk 1 back on top of Disk 2

Note that the "intermediate peg" and "destination peg" could be Peg A, Peg B, or Peg C depending on where you are in the overall process of moving the disks.

So you can use the three-step Generalized Algorithm again and again, to move as many disks as you need.

A challenging part of this Investigation is keeping track of your progress while you are in the middle of moving disks to solve the puzzle. This recursive algorithm requires you to perform tasks inside of tasks inside of tasks.
    To move all 4 disks, you will need to move 3 disks multiple times,
        and to move 3 disks, you will need to move 2 disks multiple times,
            and to move 2 disks, you will need to move the smallest disk twice.

It may help to use blank paper underneath your pegs as a scratchpad. You can keep track of what you need to do next while you solve the puzzle. For example, you could mark "3" under the peg that you want to move 3 disks to, then when you have completed that task, scratch out the 3 and write a new number for your next task.

You may cut out these strips to use as disks. This paper version views the disks from the side, so they appear as rectangles rather than circles.

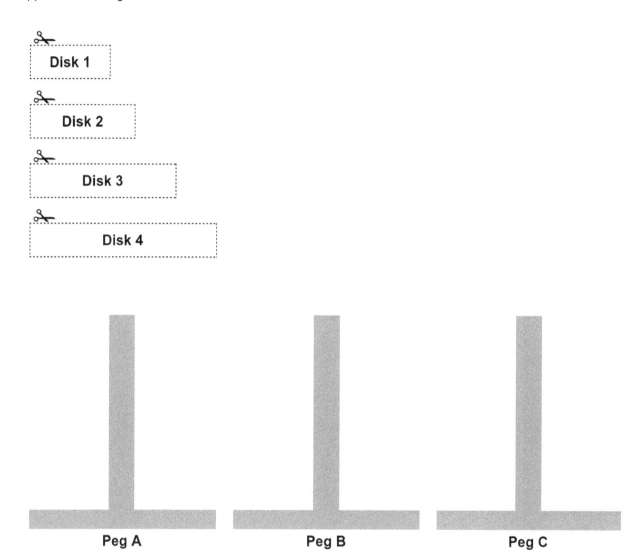

CHAPTER 6
ADD

IBM's "MIRA" supercomputer is capable of ten petaflops. One petaflop is one quadrillion (10^{15}) floating point (mathematical) operations per second.

KEY QUESTION
How can I use an algorithm to add?

OBJECTIVES
After completing this chapter, students should be able to do the following:
1. Define *base ten*, *binary*, and *logic gates*.
2. Describe the basic process a computer uses to add numbers.
3. Add two or more numbers in *base two*.
4. Write a short summary of the chapter, answering the key question.

REVIEW QUESTIONS

Answer these questions with the help of the video:

1. What are binary numbers, and why do computers use them?

_____

_____

_____

2. What is the number 1 (in base 10) written as a binary number (base two)?

_____

3. What is the number 10 (in base 10) written as a binary number (base two)?

_____

4. Explain the purpose of XOR gates in 3 to 4 sentences.

_____

_____

_____

_____

_____

_____

5. Give one new fact that you learned about computers.

_____

_____

_____

NOTES

_____

_____

_____

_____

_____

_____

_____

_____

_____

_____

_____

_____

_____

_____

_____

_____

FOR DISCUSSION
1. What kinds of things use binary (base two) instead of base ten?
2. What are the advantages of using base ten (if any)? Disadvantages (if any)?
3. What is the largest 8-digit number in base 2? What is that number in base 10?
4. How would we write 65 in binary?
6. Compare the similarities and differences of XOR, OR, and AND gates.

INVESTIGATION

For this Investigation, you will be creating and following an algorithm to add binary numbers.

1. Understand the input and output of your algorithm.

- The input will be two binary numbers.
- The output will be one binary number, which is the sum of the inputs.

2. Write a step-by-step algorithm to add two binary numbers of any length:

This will be a list of all the steps required to add two binary numbers. You can use any format you want for the steps, as long as your algorithm can be followed by someone who knows nothing about binary addition.

_____

_____

_____

_____

_____

_____

_____

_____

_____

_____

_____

3. Using your algorithm, work the following problems:

```
     101          1010101          1111111
    +11          +1100110          +101010
    ____          _____          _____
```

CHAPTER 7
DRAW

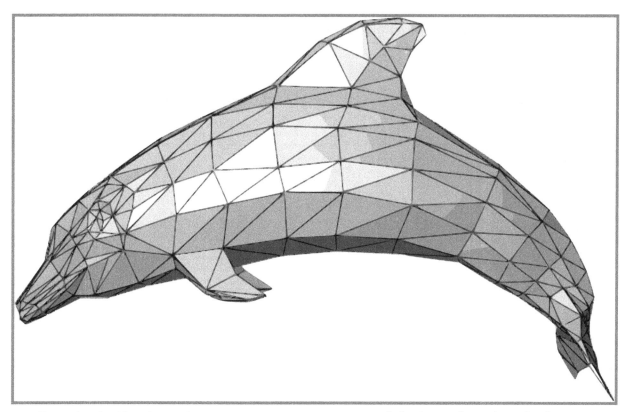

Example of a triangle mesh representing a dolphin using a relatively small number of polygons

KEY QUESTION
How can I use an algorithm to draw?

OBJECTIVES
After completing this chapter, students should be able to do the following:
1. Explain the three reasons one might use *Computer Generated Images (CGI)*.
2. Explain the benefits and the downsides of using CGI.
3. Give a simple definition of a *wireframe*.
4. Explain what *turtle graphics* are and why we use turtles.
5. Write a short summary of the chapter, answering the key question.

REVIEW QUESTIONS

Answer these questions with the help of the video:

1. What does CGI stand for?

_____

2. What are some disadvantages of using CGI instead of other methods of drawing?

_____

_____

_____

3. What are some alternatives to CGI that could be used to create images? Are these better than CGI? Why or why not?

_____

_____

_____

_____

_____

_____

4. Why was the dolphin made out of triangles? Could it be made out of other shapes? Why or why not?

_____

_____

_____

_____

_____

NOTES

DISCUSSION QUESTIONS
1. What are the advantages of using computers to draw? What are the disadvantages?
2. Why would a digital artist create a wireframe before rendering the final image?
3. What are the advantages of using triangles to create three-dimensional models?
4. Where have you seen CGI?
5. How could the dolphin be made more realistic?
6. What would be the steps to do that?

INVESTIGATION

For this Investigation you will be using a programming language called "Python" to draw your initials.

1. Understand the input and output of the algorithm you will create, as follows:
   - Input: The input will be your initials.
   - Algorithm: The algorithm will be a list of instructions for the computer to follow. The computer will interpret your algorithm and use your instructions to draw your initials.
   - Output: The output will be a computer drawing of your initials (i.e., the three letters that begin your first, middle, and last name).

2. Run a test to make sure you can run a simple Python program using your web browser, as follows:

a. Open a web browser on your computer (such as Safari or Chrome or Microsoft Edge)

b. Go to `https://trinket.io/python`

c. Click the Run icon ▶ in the toolbar, which looks like a triangle pointing to the right

If you don't see ▶ Run, you may need to click on the down arrow like this

Which should then reveal the Run option like this:

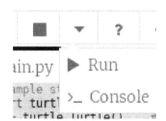

d. You should see a sample graphic being drawn on the right side of the page

This is just a quick test of trinket.io; we will replace this graphic with a new one in the next step.

e. Type the following lines and paste them into the area under "main.py" on the left side of the page.

Note that the lines below should completely replace the existing lines in the main.py window. In other words, you should delete all the text in the main.py window, and replace it with the text below.

```
# example starts here
import turtle
bob = turtle.Turtle()
bob.forward(50)
bob.right(90)
bob.forward(50)
bob.right(90)
bob.forward(50)
bob.right(90)
bob.forward(50)
# example ends here
```

f. click ► Run

You should see an arrow move on the right side of the screen, and the arrow should draw a square like this:

If you do not see a square that looks like this, you will need to fix this before continuing. You can try one or more of the following:

- Re-read the above instructions to make sure you have not skipped a step.
- Ask your instructor, fellow student, or a tech-savvy person for help.
- Try `https://skulpt.org` which is a different website that allows you to run Python code in your web browser. Type the example lines (above) into the editing window, then click "Run"
- Try `https://repl.it` which is another website for running Python code in your web browser. Click "<> start coding," choose Python, click "Create Repl," type the example lines (above) into the editing window, then click "run"

3. Now that you can draw a square using a turtle, you will move on to drawing your initials using a step-by-step algorithm in the form of a script.

The first two lines of your script should look like this. These lines create a turtle and name it "bob."

```
import turtle
bob = turtle.Turtle()
```

You can change "bob" to any name you would like for your turtle, but always include your turtle name and a period (.) before any turtle commands. Here are examples of other commands you can use:
`bob.pensize(10)`
- This determines the thickness of the pen's line. 1 is thin. 10 is thick. 15 is thicker.
`bob.penup()`
- This lifts the pen up from the page. The pen will not draw when it's up.
`bob.pendown()`
- This places the pen down on the page. The pen will now draw again.
`bob.pencolor("red")`
- This changes the color of the pen
`bob.forward(25)`
- This moves the pen forward by 25. It will draw a line if pendown() is in effect, or it will just move the pen with no line drawn if penup() is in effect.
`bob.right(90)`
- This rotates the direction of the pen by 90 degrees to the right. When the pen moves next, it will be headed in this new direction.
`bob.left(45)`
- This rotates the direction of the pen by 45 degrees to the left. When the pen moves next, it will be headed in this new direction.

Here is another example of a program that you can try if you would like to see some of the additional ways that you can control Bob the Turtle's trail.

```
# example starts here
import turtle
bob = turtle.Turtle()
bob.pensize(10)
bob.pencolor("red")
bob.forward(50)
bob.penup()
bob.forward(25)
bob.pendown()
bob.pencolor("orange")
bob.forward(50)
bob.right(90)
bob.pencolor("yellow")
bob.forward(50)
bob.penup()
bob.forward(25)
bob.pendown()
bob.pencolor("green")
bob.forward(50)
bob.right(90)
bob.pencolor("blue")
bob.forward(50)
bob.penup()
bob.forward(25)
bob.pendown()
bob.pencolor("purple")
bob.forward(50)
bob.right(90)
bob.pencolor("violet")
bob.forward(50)
bob.penup()
bob.forward(25)
bob.pendown()
bob.pencolor("brown")
bob.forward(50)
bob.right(90)
# example ends here
```

4. Create your own program that draws your initials: the first letters of your first, middle, and last names. The letters should not be connected. You can get creative with any of the following:

- Letter shapes. You can use block letters, squared-off letters, capital letters, cursive letters, 3D letters, or any shape you'd like.
- Letter colors. You can use any color or combination of colors that you wish.
- Line thickness. You can use thick lines, thin lines, or a combination.
- Fancier options (optional). You can research other ways to modify your initials, if you have the time and interest.
  - Go to `https://trinket.io/docs/python` and then click on the word "turtle." Scroll down to see all of the different functions that you can use with a turtle.

⚠ Save your program before closing your web browser, so you don't lose your work.

Save your work by copying the lines of text from your program to a word processing file, a Google Document, or a text file. To create a text file, you can use Notepad on Microsoft Windows or TextEdit on a Mac.

This will also allow you to pause and resume your work later.

Run your program at `https://trinket.io/python` to make sure it draws your initials correctly.

5. Be prepared to share your drawing with other students. Follow your instructor's process for submitting your drawing, sharing it with your group, or bringing it to your next meeting.

CHAPTER 8
VISIT

Delivery companies rely on algorithms to visit many locations as quickly as possible.

KEY QUESTION

How can I use an algorithm to visit different locations?

OBJECTIVES

After completing this chapter students should be able to do the following:

1. Describe the *Traveling Salesman Problem*.
2. Explain what a *Hamiltonian cycle* is.
3. Explain how one would use these methods: *brute force*, *nearest neighbor*, and *pairwise*.
4. Describe the difference between *weighted* and *unweighted* graphs.
5. Describe the difference between *directed* and *undirected* graphs.
6. Explain how one would use a *minimum spanning tree*.
7. Write a short summary of the chapter, answering the key question.

REVIEW QUESTIONS

Answer these questions with the help of the video:

1. Who was William Rowan Hamilton and what is a Hamiltonian Cycle?

_____

_____

_____

_____

2. When creating a Visit algorithm, when would using a heuristic be better than using the Brute Force Method? Why?

_____

_____

_____

3. What does the Minimum Spanning Tree help us accomplish?

_____

_____

_____

_____

NOTES

_____

_____

_____

_____

_____

_____

_____

_____

_____

_____

_____

_____

_____

_____

DISCUSSION QUESTIONS

1. What are different ways you could distinguish a good and bad algorithm for visiting multiple locations?
2. What types of businesses would be most interested in an algorithm for visiting different locations? Why?
3. How would you find the shortest Hamiltonian Cycle that visits the largest 10 cities in your country?

INVESTIGATION

For this Investigation you will develop an algorithm for visiting each of the Top 10 cities in Texas. You will create an algorithm and use it to follow a path that visits all 10 cities and returns to your starting city. This will be a loop, since you will have visited each city only once. You will calculate the total mileage for the complete loop. The objective is to minimize the distance that you travel.

The Top 10 Cities in Texas are as follows (ordered by population):
Houston, San Antonio, Dallas, Austin, Ft. Worth, El Paso, Arlington, Corpus Christi, Plano, and Laredo

For this Investigation, we will assume that you can only travel from a given city to a limited number of nearby other cities. For example, from El Paso you can go directly to Ft. Worth, Austin, San Antonio, or Laredo, but not directly to Houston. Below are the allowed paths between the cities and the distance for each path.
Note: You do not have to use all the paths in your complete loop. Some paths will remain unused.

You can travel either direction between cities. For example, the city pair "Austin - Houston" is listed below, but you are free to travel from Houston to Austin, not just Austin to Houston.

City Pair	Miles
El Paso - Ft. Worth	604
El Paso - Austin	576
El Paso - San Antonio	551
El Paso - Laredo	605
Laredo - San Antonio	156
Laredo - Corpus Christi	147
San Antonio - Corpus Christi	143
San Antonio - Houston	197
San Antonio - Austin	78
Austin - Houston	165
Corpus Christi - Houston	211
Austin - Arlington	202
Austin - Ft. Worth	189
Austin - Dallas	195
Dallas - Arlington	21
Ft. Worth - Arlington	15
Ft. Worth - Plano	50
Arlington - Plano	40
Plano - Dallas	20
Dallas - Houston	239

1. Understand the input and output of your algorithm

- Input
  - the distances between the cities, as shown in the list above
  - the allowed city pairs (i.e., which cities can be accessed directly from a given city).
- Output
  - the route you will take to visit all of the cities, returning to your starting city.

2. Design an algorithm for visiting each of the 10 cities using the shortest possible route.
Your algorithm should describe how to find the shortest path to visit the 10 cities.

- You must visit each city only once. You may not backtrack and land on any city twice.
- The route should return to your original city.
- You can write your algorithm under "My Visit Algorithm" on the next page.

3. Create a route using your algorithm.
The simplified map of Texas at the end of this chapter may be helpful. To aid your analysis, you can draw a diagram called an "undirected graph" or *network map*. A network map is a simple diagram representing the paths between cities and would include the following:

- Dots representing each city, labeled with the name of the city
- Lines connecting the dots, labeled with the distance between the cities it connects

Your algorithm should be generalizable and, therefore, work for visiting a different set of 10 cities. Someone should be able to use your instructions to visit any 10 cities if they know the distances between them.

My Visit Algorithm

CHAPTER 9
ENCRYPT

A telegraph can send information across distances through wires using Morse code. Morse code consists of an alphabet where each letter is transmitted using a sequence of short signals (dots) and longer signals (dashes).

KEY QUESTION
How can I use an algorithm to encrypt a message?

OBJECTIVES
After completing this chapter, students should be able to do the following:
1. Explain why someone would want to encrypt a message.
2. Define *cryptography*.
3. Define and distinguish between *codes* and *ciphers*.
4. Describe a *cipher wheel* and how it is used.
5. Describe the two kinds of ciphers talked about in this chapter.
6. Explain what it means to *encrypt* and *decrypt* something.
7. Write a short summary of the chapter, answering the key question.

REVIEW QUESTIONS

Answer these questions with the help of the video:

1. What is the etymology of the word cryptography?

_____

_____

_____

2. What are the differences between a code and a cipher?

_____

_____

3. In three to four sentences, describe a notable code or cipher.

_____

_____

_____

_____

_____

_____

4. Why are cipher wheels significant?

_____

_____

_____

5. What does Julius Caesar, who was famously assassinated in 44 BC, have to do with ciphering?

_____

_____

6. List some pros and cons of using the Vigenère cipher.

Pros: _____

Cons: _____

7. Rank the following types of ciphers from simplest to most complex:
- Single alphabet cipher
- Transformation cipher
- Polyalphabetic cipher
- Simple substitution cipher
- Vigenère cipher with an 8-letter keyword
- Caesar cipher
- Vigenère cipher with a 5-letter keyword

Simplest: _____

_____

_____

_____

_____

_____

Most complex: _____

NOTES

DISCUSSION QUESTIONS

1. Why is encryption especially important during wars?
2. What could be the consequences of poor encryption?
3. What data do you send or receive in a typical week that are encrypted?
4. Why is encryption needed for the data that you send and receive?

INVESTIGATION

For this Investigation you will use two algorithms to decrypt and encrypt messages, also known as "deciphering" and "enciphering," respectively.

1. *Decipher* the following message using a simple substitution cipher:

DULUH BUQLU JXQJJ YBBJE CEHHE MMXYZ XOEKS QDTEJ ETQON

_____

_____

It may help to track your guesses for each ciphertext letter in the list below.

Ciphertext -> Plaintext	Ciphertext -> Plaintext
A -> __	N -> __
B -> __	O -> __
C -> __	P -> __
D -> __	Q -> __
E -> __	R -> __
F -> __	S -> __
G -> __	T -> __
H -> __	U -> __
I -> __	V -> __
J -> __	W -> __
K -> __	X -> __
L -> __	Y -> __
M -> __	Z -> __

2. *Encipher* the following plaintext message using the Vigenère Cipher below:

BY FAILING TO PREPARE YOU ARE PREPARING TO FAIL

---

a. Apply the keyword to the plaintext message.
- You will use the keyword OWLS to encipher the plaintext.
- Write the first letter of the keyword (i.e, O) below the first letter (i.e., B) of your plaintext message.
- Write the second letter of the keyword below the second letter of your plaintext message.
- Write the third letter of the keyword below the third letter of your plaintext message.
- Write the fourth letter of the keyword below the fourth letter of your plaintext message.
- Write the first letter of the keyword below the fifth letter of your plaintext message.
- Continue repeating the keyword as many times as necessary to cover all the letters in your plaintext message

b. Use the tabula recta (on the next page) to encipher your message
The ***tabula recta*** is arranged like this:

	Keyword Letters
Plaintext Letters	Ciphertext Letters

Encrypt each letter of your message one-at-a-time, as follows:
- Find the first Plaintext letter in the left column of the ***tabula recta***
- Then find the corresponding Keyword letter for that Plaintext letter in the top row.
- Then find the Ciphertext letter at the intersection of that row and column.
- Write down the Ciphertext letter under the plaintext letter.
- Repeat for the next Plaintext letter in the message, until you have encrypted all the letters in the message.

Tabula Recta for using the Vigenere Cipher

Keyword Letter

	A	B	C	D	E	F	G	H	I	J	K	L	M	N	O	P	Q	R	S	T	U	V	W	X	Y	Z
A	A	B	C	D	E	F	G	H	I	J	K	L	M	N	O	P	Q	R	S	T	U	V	W	X	Y	Z
B	B	C	D	E	F	G	H	I	J	K	L	M	N	O	P	Q	R	S	T	U	V	W	X	Y	Z	A
C	C	D	E	F	G	H	I	J	K	L	M	N	O	P	Q	R	S	T	U	V	W	X	Y	Z	A	B
D	D	E	F	G	H	I	J	K	L	M	N	O	P	Q	R	S	T	U	V	W	X	Y	Z	A	B	C
E	E	F	G	H	I	J	K	L	M	N	O	P	Q	R	S	T	U	V	W	X	Y	Z	A	B	C	D
F	F	G	H	I	J	K	L	M	N	O	P	Q	R	S	T	U	V	W	X	Y	Z	A	B	C	D	E
G	G	H	I	J	K	L	M	N	O	P	Q	R	S	T	U	V	W	X	Y	Z	A	B	C	D	E	F
H	H	I	J	K	L	M	N	O	P	Q	R	S	T	U	V	W	X	Y	Z	A	B	C	D	E	F	G
I	I	J	K	L	M	N	O	P	Q	R	S	T	U	V	W	X	Y	Z	A	B	C	D	E	F	G	H
J	J	K	L	M	N	O	P	Q	R	S	T	U	V	W	X	Y	Z	A	B	C	D	E	F	G	H	I
K	K	L	M	N	O	P	Q	R	S	T	U	V	W	X	Y	Z	A	B	C	D	E	F	G	H	I	J
L	L	M	N	O	P	Q	R	S	T	U	V	W	X	Y	Z	A	B	C	D	E	F	G	H	I	J	K
M	M	N	O	P	Q	R	S	T	U	V	W	X	Y	Z	A	B	C	D	E	F	G	H	I	J	K	L
N	N	O	P	Q	R	S	T	U	V	W	X	Y	Z	A	B	C	D	E	F	G	H	I	J	K	L	M
O	O	P	Q	R	S	T	U	V	W	X	Y	Z	A	B	C	D	E	F	G	H	I	J	K	L	M	N
P	P	Q	R	S	T	U	V	W	X	Y	Z	A	B	C	D	E	F	G	H	I	J	K	L	M	N	O
Q	Q	R	S	T	U	V	W	X	Y	Z	A	B	C	D	E	F	G	H	I	J	K	L	M	N	O	P
R	R	S	T	U	V	W	X	Y	Z	A	B	C	D	E	F	G	H	I	J	K	L	M	N	O	P	Q
S	S	T	U	V	W	X	Y	Z	A	B	C	D	E	F	G	H	I	J	K	L	M	N	O	P	Q	R
T	T	U	V	W	X	Y	Z	A	B	C	D	E	F	G	H	I	J	K	L	M	N	O	P	Q	R	S
U	U	V	W	X	Y	Z	A	B	C	D	E	F	G	H	I	J	K	L	M	N	O	P	Q	R	S	T
V	V	W	X	Y	Z	A	B	C	D	E	F	G	H	I	J	K	L	M	N	O	P	Q	R	S	T	U
W	W	X	Y	Z	A	B	C	D	E	F	G	H	I	J	K	L	M	N	O	P	Q	R	S	T	U	V
X	X	Y	Z	A	B	C	D	E	F	G	H	I	J	K	L	M	N	O	P	Q	R	S	T	U	V	W
Y	Y	Z	A	B	C	D	E	F	G	H	I	J	K	L	M	N	O	P	Q	R	S	T	U	V	W	X
Z	Z	A	B	C	D	E	F	G	H	I	J	K	L	M	N	O	P	Q	R	S	T	U	V	W	X	Y

Plain-text Letter

CHAPTER 10
GUIDE

When deciding how much pasta to prepare, use 3 to 4 ounces (85 to 113 grams) of dry pasta per person.

KEY QUESTION
How can I use an algorithm to guide my decisions or actions?

OBJECTIVES
After completing this chapter, students should be able to do the following:
1. Define *heuristic*.
2. List some of the other names for heuristics.
3. List the benefits of using heuristics.
4. Describe the pitfalls of using heuristics.
5. Write a short summary of the chapter, answering the key question.

REVIEW QUESTIONS

Answer these questions with the help of the video:

1. What is a heuristic?

_____

_____

_____

2. Give 3 examples of heuristics.

_____

_____

_____

3. Where would you place your 3 examples on the private/public and informal/formal chart from Chapter 1? Why?

_____

_____

_____

_____

_____

_____

4. What are some benefits of heuristics?

_____

_____

5. What are a few of the pitfalls or disadvantages of heuristics?

_____

_____

NOTES

_____

_____

_____

_____

_____

_____

_____

_____

_____

_____

_____

_____

_____

_____

_____

_____

DISCUSSION QUESTIONS

1. What's an example of using a heuristic in the wrong way or at the wrong time?
2. What are some heuristics that you use?
3. For the heuristics that you use, where did they come from? Did you create them? Or did you learn them? If you learned them, from whom?
4. What people in your life have taught you heuristics? What are examples? How do these heuristics help you?

INVESTIGATION

In this Investigation you will discover and write down examples of at least **seven** (7) real-life heuristics that you have used. You may be using heuristics without realizing, so this Investigation may help you identify some.

- Include at least one heuristic that **estimates or approximates** something.
- Include at least one heuristic that **solves a problem**.
- Include at least one heuristic that **involves multiple steps** to get to the output.
- Include at least one heuristic that **helps you do something** in a better way.
- Include heuristics on more than one topic. Possible topics include hobbies, school, studying, work, sports, competitions, travel, and church. But don't let that list limit you.

Note: you must provide **seven (7)** total heuristics, including at least one in each of the above categories.

Below are some fill-in-the blank prompts that may help you identify heuristics. The blanks can be expanded to multiple steps or sentences as needed. You may also develop your heuristics without using these prompts.

- When dealing with _____, I've found it's helpful to do this: _____.

- To estimate _____, I can get a decent approximation by doing this: _____.

- If I want to improve _____, I've found that it helps to do this: _____.

- When I see this _____, it's a good idea not to do this: _____.

- To avoid _____, I have found that it's a good idea to do this:_____.

- When looking for _____, I can usually find it by doing this: _____.

- To do _____ quickly, I have found it helps to do this: _____.

- If I'm looking for a really good _____, I can usually find it by doing this: _____.

- To make _____, it helps if you do this: _____.

My Heuristics

1._____

_____

_____

2._____

_____

_____

3._____

_____

_____

4._____

_____

_____

5._____

_____

_____

6._____

_____

_____

7._____

_____

_____

CHAPTER 11
UNDERSTAND

A team from the International Atomic Energy Agency examines Reactor Unit 3 at the Fukushima Daiichi Nuclear Power plant in Fukushima Prefecture, Japan. It was important to understand why this reactor suffered a meltdown and explosion in March 2011.

KEY QUESTION

How can I use an algorithm to understand the root cause of a problem?

OBJECTIVES

After completing this chapter, students should be able to do the following:

1. Define "root cause."
2. Distinguish a root cause from other types of causes.
3. Use the Five Whys approach to uncover the root cause of a problem.
4. Provide examples of types of events where root cause analysis can be helpful.
5. Write a short summary of the chapter, answering the key question.

REVIEW QUESTIONS

Answer these questions with the help of the video:

1. What does RCA stand for?

_____

_____

2. Why is the Five Whys approach useful?

_____

_____

_____

3. In what situations can we apply the Five Whys?

_____

_____

_____

_____

_____

4. When looking for causes, what does the phrase "necessary, but not sufficient" mean?

_____

_____

_____

NOTES

DISCUSSION QUESTIONS

1. What are some disadvantages of using the Five Whys Approach?

2. How could the Five Whys Approach be used incorrectly or incompletely? What are the dangers?

3. What types of diagrams could be used with Root Cause Analysis? Why are these types of diagrams helpful?

4. What types of events and problems are best suited to analysis using the Five Whys Approach? Why?

5. What are examples from your own life where you could apply the Five Whys Approach?

6. How could knowing the requirements for starting a fire (i.e., fuel, oxygen, ignition) help find the Root Cause for an accidental fire?

INVESTIGATION

For this Investigation you will use the "Five Whys" process (described below) to help understand the Root Cause of two different events. You should write the output of the Five Whys process for each of the following events.

The Input is the set of events and circumstances surrounding something bad that happened.

In other words, "what happened."

The Algorithm is The Five Whys Process (described below)

The Output is a list of possible causes, including one or more "Root Causes"

In other words, "why did this happen?"

Before you investigate the two different events, let's understand the Five Whys Process and review an example of applying it.

The Five Whys Process: how to use the "Five Whys" to understand the Root Cause

Step 1. Write a one-sentence description of the problem or bad occurrence.

There are many areas where the "5 whys" approach can be useful, ranging from serious to minor. For example:

- an accident where someone is injured or killed
- a financial loss or emergency
- a near-miss where something bad almost happened
- a failure or poor result (such as a bad grade)
- a recurring unpleasantness or annoyance

The bad occurrence is the "effect" and next we will understand the causes by asking "Why?"

We want to understand the Cause-and-Effect relationship, since if we know the Cause, we can possibly prevent a re-occurrence of the Effect. The Five Whys process helps us work backwards, starting with the Effect and then uncovering the Causes.

Step 2. With respect to the bad thing that happened, ask "why did that happen?" and write the answer.

- List all the causes or reasons you can think of for the occurrence.
    - Each reason can be a short phrase or a short sentence. Keep each reason separate.
    - Think of the main reasons in this step. We will get into more detail in the next step.
- If you are having trouble answering "why did that happen?" you may wish to ask these related questions:
    - What caused this?
    - What conditions were in place to allow this to occur?
    - What decision was made that resulted in this?
- Note that there could be multiple related causes or a combination of causes. For example, a fire requires fuel, plus oxygen, plus an ignition source... all in the same location. So if your answer to "why was there a fire?" is "it was caused by a spark," then you are only partially correct. You should be able to list all the causes.
- You may end up asking more than 5 actual "why" questions. The number 5 is only a suggestion for how many questions it can take to get to the Root Cause. If you have asked only two or three why questions, then look for more complete ways to answer your previous "why" questions or consider that you may be skipping some intermediate causes.
- Consider all the prerequisites that were required for the occurrence. If you are thinking about why "Event A" happened, then ask "What is everything that needed to happen before Event A could happen?" and "What needed to be in place or present for Event A to happen?"

Step 3. For each cause or reason that you have listed, ask "why?" again for that cause, and write the answer.

Step 4. Repeat the process of asking "why?" for each cause until you have exhausted the possibilities. You should have created an outline with the main causes at the top level, then the answers to the "why?" questions forming the body of the outline, in a hierarchical, indented structure.

Step 5. Identify one or more Root Causes.
- A Root Cause is something that starts the chain of events that leads to the bad outcome. The Root Cause is the decision, action, event, or condition at the beginning of the chain of events.
- Here is a question to ask to test if you have found a Root Cause:
  - "If the Root Cause were eliminated, then would the bad outcome not have occurred?"
  - If you can answer yes, you have likely found a Root Cause.

A Five Whys Example
Here is an example of using Five Whys. This is just for your reference to see the possibilities. Your Five Whys analysis for Event 1 and Event 2 in the Investigation will have different causes.

The Problem that occurred: I spilled the milk.
The Question I want to answer: **Why** did I spill the milk?

Now think about the different things that all had to be in place or had to happen before I spilled the milk: I tripped *and* I dropped the glass, *and* the milk spilled out.
These form the three causes listed at the top level, all of which were needed for the problem to occur.
Then each of the causes has its own set of Why questions.

Cause 1: I tripped while holding the glass of milk. **Why** did I trip?
    1A. Cause: The dog ran in front of me. **Why** did the dog run in front of me?
    Cause: We allow the dog to roam freely in the house. **Why** do we allow the dog in the house?
    Cause: We have chosen to have an "inside dog." **Why** have we chosen to have an inside dog?
    Cause: We wanted a dog and our breed of dog handles the indoors better than outdoors.

    1B. Cause: I wasn't looking where I was going. **Why** wasn't I looking where I was going?
    Cause: I was paying attention to the TV across the room. **Why** was I paying attention to the TV?
    Cause: I was afraid I would miss a part of my favorite show. **Why** was I concerned about missing my show?
    Cause: The show was playing instead of being paused. **Why** was the show still playing?
    Cause: I didn't press pause when I got up to get the milk.

Cause 2: I dropped the glass containing the milk. **Why** did I drop the glass?
    Cause: I didn't have a good grip on the glass. **Why** did I not have a good grip on the glass?
    Cause: The shape of the glass: it was large, smooth, and without a handle. **Why** is the glass shaped the way it is?
    Cause: That's the one we chose and bought at the store. **Why** is that the one you chose and bought?
    Cause: That's the only one that matches our plates. **Why** is it the only one that matches our plates?
    Cause: There were not many types to choose from at the store.

Cause 3: The milk spilled over the top of the glass. **Why** did the milk spill out of the glass?
    Cause: I was using a glass that did not have a lid. **Why** was I drinking from a glass without a lid?
    Cause: I'm not a baby and I don't use a sippy cup. **Why** don't you use a spill-proof cup?
    Cause: I don't like them. **Why** do I not like spill-proof cups?

Cause: It's too inconvenient to drink from a spill-proof cup, and they're expensive.

What is the Root Cause (or causes)?
Looking at the list of causes above, there are several possibilities, including the following:
- Having a dog in the kitchen
  - Possible solution = keep the dog out of the kitchen, where he is more likely to get into the way
- Not pressing pausing on the TV when you leave the room
  - Possible solution = pause the TV when you go to the kitchen to get a snack
  - This one has a simple solution that merely requires a simple change in behavior.
- Not using a spill-proof cup
  - Possible solution = find an easy-to-use, spill-proof cup

Now you can apply the Five Whys Process to specific events.

Event 1: An event of your choice when you missed a deadline or when you were late for an appointment.
- Think of a time in your life, within the last year, when you were late for a commitment or missed a deadline.
- Follow the Five Whys process to find the Root Cause of the problem or bad occurrence.
- Write down your answers to the Five Whys process below. List the Root Cause (or causes).

Event 2: A specific airplane crash that occurred in 2009.

- The facts relating to the crash are described in the NTSB "Factual Report" on the following pages.
- Read the report and follow the Five Whys process to find the Root Cause of the problem or bad occurrence.
- If you don't know the exact answer to a Why question, you may need to estimate or use your best guess.
- Write down your answers to the Five Whys process below. List the Root Cause (or causes).

National Transportation Safety Board **FACTUAL REPORT AVIATION**	NTSB ID: CEN09FA369	Aircraft Registration Number: N182GT
	Occurrence Date: 06/18/2009	Most Critical Injury: Fatal
	Occurrence Type: Accident	Investigated By: NTSB

Location/Time

Nearest City/Place	State	Zip Code	Local Time	Time Zone	
Dougherty	TX	79231	2138	CDT	

Airport Proximity: Off Airport/Airstrip	Distance From Landing Facility:

Aircraft Information Summary

Aircraft Manufacturer	Model/Series	Type of Aircraft
CESSNA	R182	Airplane

Revenue Sightseeing Flight: No	Air Medical Transport Flight: No

Narrative

Brief narrative statement of facts, conditions and circumstances pertinent to the accident/incident:

*** Note: NTSB investigators either traveled in support of this investigation or conducted a significant amount of investigative work without any travel, and used data obtained from various sources to prepare this aircraft accident report. ***

HISTORY OF FLIGHT

On June 18, 2009, at 2138 central daylight time, a Cessna R182, N182GT, piloted by a private pilot, was destroyed when it impacted terrain two miles north of Dougherty, Texas. A post impact fire ensued. Night instrument meteorological conditions prevailed at the time of the accident. The personal flight was being conducted under the provisions of Title 14 Code of Federal Regulation Part 91 without a flight plan. The pilot and pilot rated passenger were both fatally injured. The cross-country flight departed Houston Southwest Airport (KAXH), Houston, Texas, and was en route to Hale County Airport (KPVW), Plainview, Texas.

According to the UNICOM operator at KPVW, a female had contacted him via telephone earlier in the day to ensure that someone would be at the airport when they arrived later that evening. Approximately 2125 the pilot called the UNICOM frequency asking which runway was in use. Approximately 2140, the pilot called the UNICOM frequency again, asking about the weather at KPVW. The UNICOM operator attempted to contact the accident airplane at 2150 with no response.

Radar data, provided by the Federal Aviation Administration (FAA) in National Track Analysis Program (NTAP) format, depicted the accident flight from 2115 to the time of the accident. The airplane was at an encoded altitude of 6,400 feet on a north, northwesterly heading. The airplane track reversed course to a south, southeasterly heading and descended to an altitude of 6,000 feet. The airplane track reversed course again to a north, northwesterly track and climbed to an altitude of 6,500 feet. The airplane track changed a third time to an easterly heading, and then a fourth time to a westerly heading. The last radar return was recorded at 2138:19, 4,256 feet from the location of the main wreckage.

The airplane wreckage was located in a field on June 20, 2009, by a local resident.

PERSONNEL INFORMATION

The pilot, age 53, held a private pilot certificate with airplane single engine land privileges, last issued on March 8, 2007. He was issued a third class airman medical certificate on October 20, 2008. The certificate contained the limitation "must wear lenses for distant - possess glasses for near vision."

The pilot's flight logbook was located within the wreckage. A review of the logbook indicated that the pilot had logged no less than 412 hours; 45.5 hours in the make and model of the accident airplane, 17.7 hours at night, and 4.6 hours in simulated instrument meteorological conditions.

National Transportation Safety Board **FACTUAL REPORT** **AVIATION**	NTSB ID: CEN09FA369
	Occurrence Date: 06/18/2009
	Occurrence Type: Accident

Narrative (Continued)

The pilot had logged 52.8 and 20.1 hours within the previous 90 and 30 days respectively. The pilot had logged 4.4 hours of night experience within the previous 90 days and 1.1 hours within the previous 30 days.

The pilot successfully completed the requirements of a flight review as required by CFR 61.56 on April 11, 2009. He received training in the Cessna 182 RG and obtained both a high performance and complex airplane endorsement on May 3, 2009.

The pilot rated passenger held a private pilot certificate; however, her medical certificate was not current. Flight time and experience for the passenger was not evaluated.

AIRCRAFT INFORMATION

The accident airplane, a Cessna R182 (serial number R18201504), was manufactured in 1980. It was registered with the FAA on a standard airworthiness certificate for normal operations. A Lycoming O-540 engine rated at 250 horsepower at 2,400 rpm powered the airplane. The engine was equipped with a two-blade, McCauley propeller.

The airplane was registered to and operated by the pilot, and was maintained under an annual inspection program. The maintenance records were not located. An invoice provided by Parker Aircraft LLC indicated that an annual inspection had been billed for on October 21, 2008. An additional maintenance entry was provided by another mechanic indicating general maintenance had been performed on April 10, 2009, at a tachometer time of 3,056.0 hours.

METEOROLOGICAL CONDITIONS

The synoptic conditions over the Texas were favorable for high-based thunderstorms development during the afternoon and evening hours on June 18, 2209. The National Weather Service (NWS) Storm Prediction Center's Convective Outlook had expected a slight risk of severe thunderstorm development over the region and had issued an advisory for a line of thunderstorms over the Texas panhandle with the threat of strong locally damaging winds. The NWS Radar Summary Chart for 2120 depicted a solid line of thunderstorms west and northwest of the accident site, with the 2200 Surface Analysis Chart depicting an outflow boundary bowing outwards over western Texas, and the Texas panhandle, in the immediate vicinity of the accident site.

The Lubbock 1900 upper air sounding data depicted a warm dry low-level environment with an elevated lifted condensation level (LCL) and level of free convection (LFC) favorable for high-based convection. The sounding provided a Lifted Index of -6.3 and a K-Index of 40, which indicated an unstable atmosphere and a high probability of thunderstorms, with conditions also favorable for strong outflow winds and microbursts.

Geostationary Operations Environmental Satellite (GOES) imagery (visible and infrared) was obtained for the time period surrounding the accident. The data depicted cumulonimbus clouds to the northwest of the accident site. A cumulonimbus anvil cloud and middle level clouds were depicted directly above the accident site.

The Lubbock Doppler weather radar (WSR-88D) depicted a large area of echoes over the Texas panhandle with maximum reflectivity of 61 dBZ and intense to extreme precipitation along the leading edge, northwest of the accident site. A fine line was identified ahead of the band of echoes associated with an outflow boundary or gust front that was oriented in a north south direction was depicted moving through the accident site between 2135 and 2140.

The NWS had several Convective SIGMETs (Significant Airman's Meteorological Information) valid for areas north, south, and west of the accident site. Convective SIGMET 16C and 17 C warned of several areas of severe thunderstorms moving from 240 degrees at 30 knots, with cloud tops above 45,000 feet, and warned of potential hail to 1 inch and wind gusts to 70 knots. The advisory also implied severe to extreme turbulence, lightning, low-level wind shear, and localized instrument meteorological conditions were possible.

National Transportation Safety Board **FACTUAL REPORT AVIATION**	NTSB ID: CEN09FA369
	Occurrence Date: 06/18/2009
	Occurrence Type: Accident

Narrative   (Continued)

There were no AIRMETS that impacted the route of flight.

The closest official weather observation station was Hale County Airport (KPVW), located in Plainview, Texas, 34 nautical miles (nm) northwest of the accident site at an elevation of 3,374 feet. The observations for KPVW reported strong southerly winds shifting to the west with the passage of the outflow boundary. At 2125 KPVW reported wind from 270 degrees at 18 knots gusting to 33 knots, visibility 2 ½ miles in heavy rain, scattered clouds at 800 feet agl, ceiling broken at 5,000 feet, overcast at 6,500 feet, temperature 19 degrees Celsius (C), dew point 17 degrees C, altimeter setting 29.97 inches of Mercury (Hg). The remarks indicated surface visibility varied from 1 ¾ to 5 miles. At 2145 KPVW reported, wind 270 degrees at 19 knots, gusting to 22 knots, visibility 10 miles in light rain, scattered clouds at 1,100 feet, ceiling broken 10,000 feet, overcast 11,000 feet, temperature 18 degrees C, dew point 17 degrees C, and altimeter 29.94 inches of Hg.

The next closet weather observation station was Lubbock Preston Smith International Airport (KLBB), Lubbock, Texas, located 40 miles west-southwest of the accident site at an elevation of 3,282 feet msl. Lubbock also reported a wind shift from the south to the west at 2040 with wind gusts to 51 knots and visibility ¾ of a mile in blowing dust, followed by light rain and thunderstorms. At 2102 a special observation at KLBB reported, winds 280 degrees at 25 knots, gusting to 35 knots, visibility 4 miles in blowing dust, scattered 3,000 feet agl, ceiling broken at 6,000 feet, overcast at 12,000 feet, temperature 22 degrees C, dew point 16 degrees, and altimeter 29.91 inches of Hg. The remarks section reported a peak wind gust of 35 knots at 2055 CDT, with cumulonimbus clouds in the distance west through northwest, moving northeast.

According to the United States Naval Observatory, Astronomical Applications Department Sun and Moon Data, the sunset was recorded at 2100 and the end of civil twilight was 2129. The moon rose at 0608 and set at 2119 on the day of the accident.

Two witnesses in the area at the time of the accident described wind speeds between 60 and 70 miles per hour, and blowing dust and dirt, consistent with a windstorm and brownout conditions.

There was no record of the pilot obtaining a formal weather briefing from the FAA Automated Flight Service Station (AFSS) or the Direct User Access Terminal Service (DUATS).

WRECKAGE AND IMPACT INFORMATION

The accident scene was located in a dormant cotton field at a field elevation of 3,100 feet msl. The wreckage was fragmented and consisted of fragments of the left and right wing assemblies, empennage, fuselage, and engine assembly.

A ground scar two feet wide and 25 feet long characterized the initial impact point that terminated at a large impact crater. Dirt and debris was pushed out of the large crater in the direction of impact. The crater was three to four feet deep and contained fragmented remains on instruments, engine hoses, and wires. The engine and propeller assembly was partially buried in this hole with the lowest end at a depth of six feet.

A debris path extended from the impact crater in an easterly direction towards the main wreckage. The path was 85 feet wide by 138 feet long and contained the fragmented remains of engine accessories, hoses, wires, both the left and right wing assemblies, and various cabin components.

The main wreckage consisted of the bent and burned remains of the empennage, fuselage, and forward cockpit and cabin area. Rudder and elevator cables were continuous from the forward fuselage aft to their respective termination points in the empennage. Aileron cables were continuous; however, several points of separation were noted with features consistent with overload separation. Debris fanned out from the main wreckage for an additional 250 feet.

The engine was recovered from the impact crater. The propeller assembly remained attached and both propeller blades were bent aft 90 degrees around the engine housing. Both blades exhibited leading and trailing edge polishing and chordwise scratches on the blade face. The engine could not be rotated through due to impact damage.

National Transportation Safety Board **FACTUAL REPORT AVIATION**	NTSB ID: CEN09FA369	
	Occurrence Date: 06/18/2009	
	Occurrence Type: Accident	

Narrative   (Continued)

A bore scope examination of each cylinder revealed signatures consistent with normal operation. Engine accessories were destroyed and their functionality could not be established.

MEDICAL AND PATHOLOGICAL INFORMATION

An autopsy was performed on the pilot by the Texas Tech University Health Sciences Center - Division of Forensic Pathology, Lubbock, Texas, on June 22, 2009, as authorized by the Justice of the Peace in Floyd County. The autopsy concluded that the cause of death was "blunt force injuries."

During the autopsy, specimens were collected for toxicological testing to be performed by the FAA's Civil Aerospace Medical Institute, Oklahoma City, Oklahoma (CAMI Reference #200900135002). No blood was received by the FAA laboratory and tests for carbon monoxide and cyanide were not performed. Ethanol and propanol were detected in the liver, muscle, and kidney tissue. Methanol was detected in the liver and butanol was detected in the muscle. Results were negative for drugs.

The wreckage was discovered two days following the accident and there was a delay in the recovery of the bodies. Putrefaction was noted on the toxicology report.
Updated on Apr 22 2010 4:51PM

National Transportation Safety Board **FACTUAL REPORT AVIATION**	NTSB ID: CEN09FA369
	Occurrence Date: 06/18/2009
	Occurrence Type: Accident

Landing Facility/Approach Information

Airport Name	Airport ID:	Airport Elevation Ft. MSL	Runway Used N/A	Runway Length	Runway Width

Runway Surface Type:

Runway Surface Condition:

Approach/Arrival Flown: NONE

VFR Approach/Landing: None

Aircraft Information

Aircraft Manufacturer CESSNA	Model/Series R182	Serial Number R18201504

Airworthiness Certificate(s): Normal

Landing Gear Type: Retractable - Tricycle

Amateur Built Acft? No	Number of Seats: 4	Certified Max Gross Wt.	LBS	Number of Engines: 1

Engine Type: Reciprocating	Engine Manufacturer: LYCOMING	Model/Series: O-540 SERIES	Rated Power: 250 HP

- Aircraft Inspection Information

Type of Last Inspection Annual	Date of Last Inspection 12/2008	Time Since Last Inspection Hours	Airframe Total Time Hours

- Emergency Locator Transmitter (ELT) Information

ELT Installed?/Type Yes /	ELT Operated?	ELT Aided in Locating Accident Site? No

Owner/Operator Information

Registered Aircraft Owner Rainer Aberer	Street Address 7447 CAMBRIDGE ST APT 70		
	City HOUSTON	State TX	Zip Code 77054-2019

Operator of Aircraft Rainer Aberer	Street Address 7447 CAMBRIDGE ST APT 70		
	City HOUSTON	State TX	Zip Code 77054-2019

Operator Does Business As: | Operator Designator Code:

- Type of U.S. Certificate(s) Held: None

Air Carrier Operating Certificate(s):

Operating Certificate:	Operator Certificate:

Regulation Flight Conducted Under: Part 91: General Aviation

Type of Flight Operation Conducted: Personal

National Transportation Safety Board **FACTUAL REPORT AVIATION**	NTSB ID: CEN09FA369	
	Occurrence Date: 06/18/2009	
	Occurrence Type: Accident	

First Pilot Information

Name		City		State	Date of Birth	Age
On File		On File		On File	On File	53

Sex: M	Seat Occupied: Unknown	Occupational Pilot? No		Certificate Number: On File

Certificate(s):   Private

Airplane Rating(s):   Single-engine Land

Rotorcraft/Glider/LTA: None

Instrument Rating(s): None

Instructor Rating(s): None

Current Biennial Flight Review? 04/2009

Medical Cert.: Class 3	Medical Cert. Status: With Waivers/Limitations	Date of Last Medical Exam: 10/2008

- Flight Time Matrix	All A/C	This Make and Model	Airplane Single Engine	Airplane Mult-Engine	Night	Instrument Actual	Instrument Simulated	Rotorcraft	Glider	Lighter Than Air
Total Time	412	45			17					
Pilot In Command(PIC)										
Instructor										
Instruction Received										
Last 90 Days	53				4					
Last 30 Days	20				1					
Last 24 Hours										

Seatbelt Used? Yes	Shoulder Harness Used? Yes	Toxicology Performed? Yes	Second Pilot? Yes

Flight Plan/Itinerary

Type of Flight Plan Filed: None

Departure Point		State	Airport Identifier	Departure Time	Time Zone
Houston		TX	KAHX		

Destination		State	Airport Identifier		
Plainview		TX	KPVW		

Type of Clearance: None

Type of Airspace:

Weather Information

Pilot's Source of Wx Information:

National Transportation Safety Board **FACTUAL REPORT AVIATION**	NTSB ID: CEN09FA369
	Occurrence Date: 06/18/2009
	Occurrence Type: Accident

Weather Information

WOF ID	Observation Time	Time Zone	WOF Elevation	WOF Distance From Accident Site	Direction From Accident Site
PVW	2245	CDT	Ft. MSL	34 NM	330 Deg. Mag.

Sky/Lowest Cloud Condition: Scattered	1100 Ft. AGL	Condition of Light: Night

Lowest Ceiling: Broken	10000 Ft. AGL	Visibility:	10	SM	Altimeter:	29.94	"Hg

Temperature:	18 °C	Dew Point:	17 °C	Weather Conditions at Accident Site: Instrument Conditions

Wind Direction: 270	Wind Speed: 19	Wind Gusts: 22

Visibility (RVR):	Ft.	Visibility (RVV)	SM	

Precip and/or Obscuration:

Accident Information

Aircraft Damage: Destroyed	Aircraft Fire: Ground	Aircraft Explosion None

- Injury Summary Matrix	Fatal	Serious	Minor	None	TOTAL
First Pilot	1				1
Second Pilot					
Student Pilot					
Flight Instructor					
Check Pilot					
Flight Engineer					
Cabin Attendants					
Other Crew					
Passengers	1				1
- TOTAL ABOARD -	2				2
Other Ground					
- GRAND TOTAL -	2				2

National Transportation Safety Board	NTSB ID: CEN09FA369	
FACTUAL REPORT	Occurrence Date: 06/18/2009	
AVIATION	Occurrence Type: Accident	

Administrative Information

Investigator-In-Charge (IIC)

Jennifer Rodi

Additional Persons Participating in This Accident/Incident Investigation:

Arturo   Castillo
FAA Flight Standards District Office
Lubbock, TX

Steve   Miller
Cessna Aircraft Company
Wichita, KS

John   Butler
Lycoming Engines
Arlington, TX

CHAPTER 12

DIAGRAM

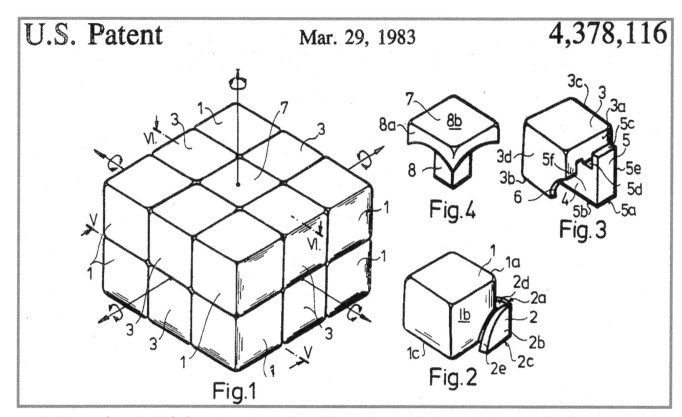

U.S. Patent — Mar. 29, 1983 — 4,378,116

Fig.1 Fig.2 Fig.3 Fig.4

A diagram from the U.S. Patent application for a "Spatial Logical Toy," invented by Ernö Rubik of Budapest, Hungary.

KEY QUESTION

How can I use an algorithm to create a diagram?

OBJECTIVES

After completing this chapter, students should be able to do the following:

1. Identify different types of diagrams and explain their usefulness.
2. Create a *flowchart* to model a sequence of events.
3. Create a *network diagram* or *tree* to show the relationships between things.
4. Write a short summary of the chapter, answering the key question.

REVIEW QUESTIONS

Answer these questions with the help of the video:

1. What are some types of relationships that a diagram can help us understand?

_____

_____

_____

_____

2. How could each of these elements be useful when creating a diagram?

Shapes: _____

Lines: _____

Labels: _____

Colors: _____

Arrows: _____

3. What is mind-mapping, and what can it help us to do?

_____

_____

_____

_____

NOTES

_____

_____

_____

_____

_____

_____

_____

_____

_____

_____

_____

_____

_____

_____

DISCUSSION QUESTIONS

1. Is a diagram itself an algorithm? Why or why not?
2. Have you ever purchased something that included a diagram in the instructions? If so, what? Was the diagram helpful? Why or why not?
3. Which of the diagrams described in this chapter seem the most useful to you? Why?
4. What kinds of diagrams could help you with your schoolwork or with studying for tests?
5. How can we choose the best level of abstraction for a diagram? In other words, how should we choose which details to include and which to omit?

INVESTIGATION

In this Investigation you will create three separate diagrams to describe a process, a network, and a collection of things. Use the space under each description to draw your diagram. If you run out of space, you can use a separate sheet.

Diagram 1: Draw a process flowchart that describes how to safely cross a street that has a crosswalk button.

- Begin with a "Start" symbol, which is an oval: ◯
- End with an "End" symbol, which is an oval: ◯
- Use the following symbols as many times as needed:
  - a process step should be enclosed by a rectangle: ▢
  - a waiting step should be enclosed by a circle ◯
  - a decision step should be enclosed by a diamond ◇
- Test the accuracy and completeness of your flowchart by imagining that you are at the "Start" step, and then follow the steps until you have crossed the street. Make sure that someone could follow your process flowchart and cross the street safely.

Diagram 2: Draw a network map that describes your home.

This diagram will be a set of connected dots, where each dot represents an area in your home.

- Create a node for each exterior door (i.e., a door that leads to the outside)
  - Draw a dot for each node.
- Create a node for each accessible space or area inside your home (i.e., room, closet, hallway).
  - Label each node with the name of the room or area
- If your home has multiple floors, create one node for each set of stairs.
  - Then use that stair node to connect the two floors.
  - Your diagram will have a section for each floor of your home, and each section will be connected to the stairs node.
- Connect adjacent nodes with a line.
  - Connect the dots with lines that touch the dots.
  - A node can be adjacent to multiple other nodes. For example, a kitchen node might connect to a dining room, pantry, and back door.
  - Connect the exterior door nodes to the appropriate rooms.
  - All nodes should be connected with a line to at least one other node.

Diagram 3: Draw a tree diagram that describes a McDonald's Happy Meal.

This diagram will describe a Happy Meal with the Hamburger Entrée (not a Cheeseburger or McNuggets). If you are not familiar with the contents of a Happy Meal, you can research this online at `https://www.mcdonalds.com` or other sites. Note that the McDonald's site and accompanying photos do not describe the Happy Meal packaging or the Happy Meal toy.

- The topmost node in your tree diagram should be "Happy Meal."
- Create nodes for every item that makes up a Happy Meal, including all packaging.
  - An "item" is something which can be separated from the other items and is distinctly identifiable, such as a side item, a drink, a toy, or a wrapper.
  - Draw each node as a dot on your page. Label each node.
- Some "parent" items can be further broken down into more "child" items. For example, a hamburger has several separable ingredients such as a beef patty and pickle. For these items that have multiple component parts, draw a separate node for each child item under the parent node and connect the child to its parent.
- Continue to add nodes for each item and add nodes for each child until you can no longer identify separate child items.
  - For example, "ketchup" is as far as you need to go, since you can't physically separate the ketchup ingredients such as tomatoes, vinegar, sugar, and salt.

CHAPTER 13
BRAINSTORM

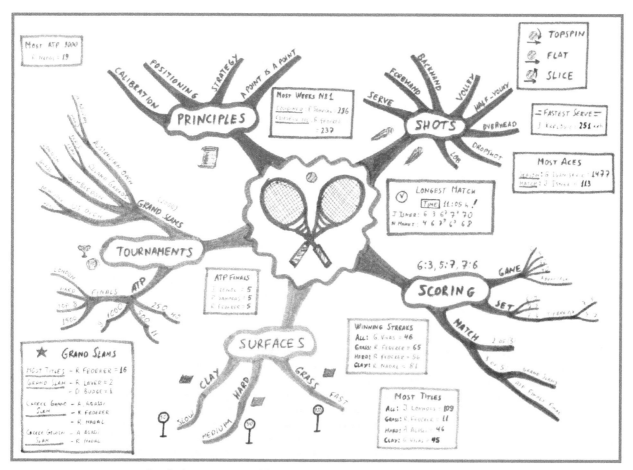

A mind map created by brainstorming ideas about tennis.

KEY QUESTION
How can I use an algorithm to brainstorm new ideas?

OBJECTIVES
After completing this chapter, students should be able to do the following:
1. Describe how to brainstorm new ideas by oneself.
2. Describe ways to brainstorm new ideas as part of a group.
3. Describe the *LATCH* framework.
4. Write a short summary of the chapter, answering the key question.

REVIEW QUESTIONS

Answer these questions with the help of the video:

1. List three reasons one might brainstorm.

_____

_____

_____

2. What are some different types of brainstorming? What are the pros and cons of each?

_____

_____

_____

_____

_____

_____

3. Create a mindmap with ideas for a new book on any topic you choose.

NOTES

_____

_____

_____

_____

_____

_____

_____

_____

_____

_____

_____

_____

_____

_____

_____

_____

DISCUSSION QUESTIONS

1. What's an example of a topic you have brainstormed in the past? Did you generate enough ideas? If you could brainstorm that topic again, what would you do differently?

2. What do you think is easier: brainstorming in a group, or brainstorming by yourself? Why? What examples can you provide?

3. What occupations would require a lot of brainstorming? For what purpose? Would you enjoy working at that job? Why or why not?

4. What is a situation in your life where you don't have as many ideas as you would like? Could brainstorming help? Why or why not?

INVESTIGATION

In this Investigation you will brainstorm *four* different topics, resulting in four different sets of ideas. For topic #1, you will generate a list of at least 20 ideas. For topics #2, #3, and #4, you will brainstorm ideas, and then pick your best one. Note: you need to develop complete and submit answers to *all four* of the brainstorm investigations below.

Brainstorm #1

List all the tips, techniques, suggestions, and ideas that you can think of related to this topic:
"How to achieve a great score on an upcoming math test"
Or if you prefer, you can choose "How to achieve a great score on an upcoming standardized test" (e.g., PSAT, SAT, or ACT)

- Use the LATCH framework to generate ideas. Generate *at least two* ideas for each of the five letters in LATCH.
- Generate at least 20 ideas in total, but you are welcome to develop more than 20.
- Each idea can be brief: one or two sentences. Each idea should be a complete sentence.
- You may brainstorm other ideas, even if they do not fit in the LATCH framework. You can use brainstorming methods from the video lesson, or any other helpful technique.
- You may include ideas that could help with preparing for any test, but focus your attention on specific advice for your upcoming test.
- The sentence patterns below may help you with brainstorming, but these are just suggestions:
    - Based on similar tests in the past, I wish someone had told me how to _____.
    - My advice to other students taking the test would be _____.
    - Students who do well on this type of test usually do _____.
    - Students who do well on this type of test usually do not _____.
    - Students who do poorly on this type of test usually do _____.
    - Based on similar tests in the past, _____ can help you prepare.
    - During the test, you need to do _____.
    - I tend to do well on _____ topic, and a suggestion for someone else wanting to do well on that topic would be to _____.
    - A difficult part of the test will probably be _____, and a way to make that easier is _____.

- If there are topics on the test that may be particularly challenging (or unsuccessful) for you, then brainstorm ways that you could be more successful in those areas prior to taking the test.

20 ideas for "How to achieve a great score on an upcoming math test"

1. _____

2. _____

3. _____

4. _____

5. _____

6. _____

7. _____

8. _____

9. _____

10. _____

11. _____

12. _____

13. _____

14. _____

15. _____

16. _____

17. _____

18. _____

19. _____

20. _____

Brainstorm #2

Generate ideas and then choose your best one to complete the following sentence:

"A good idea for a physical product that I could create and sell is _____. "

- A **physical product** is a thing that you could make or assemble from ingredients, inputs, or raw materials. Your product can also be something that you refine, develop, or grow.
- Physical products are things that need to be shipped or delivered, not downloaded.
- Use the LATCH framework or any other method you wish to generate ideas.
- Your product prototype should cost less than $250 for you to create.
    - The total cost of your raw materials and supplies for this product should cost less than $250.
    - To make your product, you can use equipment that costs more than $250, as long as you plan to borrow or rent the equipment instead of buying it.
    - Your time and effort is not counted as part of the $250.
    - If you get free help or advice, that doesn't count as part of the $250
- Remember that you are just brainstorming ideas; you do not actually need to make this product.
- Be prepared to explain how you came up with your idea.
- Be prepared to explain why your idea is a good one.
- You are not required to submit your full brainstormed list, just your best idea.

A good idea for a physical product that I could provide and sell is

_____

_____

_____

Brainstorm #3

Generate ideas and then choose your best one to complete the following sentence:
"A good idea for an information product that I could create and sell is _____."

- An "**information product**" is some useful or interesting knowledge that can be shared with others.
    - The purpose of an information product can be entertainment, education, or work. Information products can take various forms such as images, video, text, audio, a live event, a performance, or a combination of these.
    - Some information products are delivered in a digital format that can be downloaded or streamed.
    - Some information products are delivered using physical media such as paper, canvas, compact disc, DVD, or film.
    - Some information products are delivered live and in-person, like at a concert, class, event, or training session.
- Use the LATCH framework or any other method you wish to generate ideas.
- Be prepared to explain the process by which you came up with your idea and why you think it is good.
- You are not required to submit your full brainstormed list, just your best idea.

A good idea for an information product that I could provide and sell is

_____

_____

_____

Brainstorm #4

Generate ideas and then choose your best one to complete the following sentence:

"A good idea for a service that I could provide and sell is _____."

- A **service** is something you can do or an action you can take to help others. A "pure service" does not involve providing a physical product, but some services include a complimentary product. For example, an auto mechanic might provide oil as part of an oil change service. Or a tutor might provide some worksheets or review sheets as part of the tutoring service. The service you choose can be a pure service, or it can have a product associated with it.
- Use the LATCH framework or any other method you wish to generate ideas.
- Be prepared to explain the process by which you came up with your idea and why you think it is good.
- You are not required to provide your full brainstormed list, just your best idea.

A good idea for a service that I could provide and sell is

_____

_____

_____

CHAPTER 14
VALIDATE

A 1958 Ford Edsel Ranger 4-Door Sedan. Due to an inadequate market validation process, this car was not what buyers wanted, and the company lost $250 million on the project.

KEY QUESTION

How can I use an algorithm to validate my idea?

OBJECTIVES

After completing this chapter, students should be able to do the following:
1. Explain how to *validate* an idea, and why validation is important.
2. Explain how to use the *scientific method* to validate an idea.
3. Explain how to use *A/B testing* to validate an idea.
4. Describe the purpose of the Lean Canvas.
5. Explain how to use the *Lean Canvas* to validate an idea.
6. Write a short summary of the chapter, answering the key question.

REVIEW QUESTIONS

Answer these questions with the help of the video:

1. In your opinion, what are the factors that determine the validity of an idea or product?

_____

_____

_____

_____

_____

2. What are some examples of validation processes (or validation algorithms)?

_____

_____

_____

3. For a validation test, what is the Input, Algorithm, and Output?

_____

_____

_____

4. Explain A/B testing and acceptance testing.

_____

_____

_____

5. What does the Lean Canvas help accomplish?

_____

_____

_____

_____

6. What does MVP mean (in the context of this chapter) and how does it relate to algorithms? (Hint: it doesn't stand for Most Valuable Player)

_____

_____

_____

_____

_____

_____

NOTES

_____

_____

_____

_____

_____

_____

_____

_____

_____

_____

_____

_____

_____

_____

_____

_____

DISCUSSION QUESTIONS

1. What types of business ideas might not be suited to using the Lean Canvas approach? Why?

2. What types of products should use acceptance testing (other than cars, planes, and software)? What are the most important things the testers should look for?

3. If you were writing an algorithm to validate a new food that you invented, what would be the main features of that algorithm? Where would you find people to test your food? What questions would you ask them?

INVESTIGATION

In this Investigation you will use an algorithm that helps validate (or invalidate!) a business idea. We will use the Lean Canvas and the Minimum Viable Product approach. Follow the steps below to complete this Investigation.

Step 1. Pick an idea that you have for selling something. Your idea should be one of the following:
- a physical product (see Chapter 13 Investigation, Brainstorm #2)
- an information product (see Chapter 13 Investigation, Brainstorm #3)
- a service (see Chapter 13 Investigation, Brainstorm #4)
- a blend of these.

Your idea should be something that you have brainstormed previously. Pick an idea that is theoretically possible for you to pursue with limited funds (e.g., $200 or less). This idea will be the "Solution" that we will use in the next step.

Step 2. Fill in the Lean Canvas for your idea.

Use the 1-page Lean Canvas at the end of this chapter. Remove the page from this book if that makes it easier for you to write on the page.

Fill in the sections on the page in the order below. Note: the order is not left-to-right. Use the descriptions and answer the questions below to fill in each section. Write your answers on the Lean Canvas page or on a separate sheet if you need more space. If your chosen idea is not working very well, you can return to your list of brainstormed ideas and choose another idea.

1a. Customer Segments
> Who are your target customers and users? Describe your primary targets (i.e., your ideal, eager customers) and secondary targets (i.e., people who are interested, but less eager).

1b. Early Adopters.
> What are the characteristics of your ideal, most eager customers? List who they are, what they do, and what they like.

2a. Problem
> What are your prospective customers' Top 3 problems that your solution will solve?

2b. Existing Alternatives
> How do your prospective customers solve these Top 3 problems today?

3a. Unique Value Proposition (UVP)
> What is your single, clear, compelling message that states why you are different and worth paying attention to? This should be 15 words or less.
>
> You can use any format for your Unique Value Proposition, but it may be helpful to use one of these patterns:
>> We help **_my target customer_** do **_a top problem to solve_** by doing **_my solution_**.
>>> We help busy moms get more free time by running errands for them.
>>> We help Christian families educate their children by providing classical, core courses.
>>> We help farmers increase crop yield by using a satellite-guided fertilization system.
>>> We help companies of all sizes transform how people connect, communicate, and collaborate. (Cisco Systems)
>> The **_superlative adjective_** way to **_verb_**
>>> The best free way to manage your expenses.

The fastest way to fix your iPhone.

It's Not Just Easy, It's GEICO Easy

This is another way of saying "The easiest way to switch insurance companies."

All the News That's Fit to Print (The New York Times)

This is another way of saying "The most complete way to get your news."

The Quicker Picker Upper (Bounty Paper Towels)

This is another way of saying "The quicker way to pick up your mess."

Verb your **_noun_**

Grow your business.

Share your best moments.

Accomplish your personal projects.

Raise money for your charity.

Verb more **_noun_**

Find more customers.

Get more free time.

Adjective adjective noun

Cable-free live TV is here. (YouTube TV)

The World's Best Long Haul, Low-Cost Airline (Norwegian Air)

Finally, a way to **verb phrase**.

Finally, a way to invest in blockchain.

3b. High-level concept. This step is optional since it might not apply to your idea. But see if you can find one that fits your idea.

If you are applying an existing concept to a new area, you can use an analogy in the form of "X for Y" to help people understand what you do. X is an existing business and Y is a new area where that business idea can be applied. For example,

- YouTube could be described as "Flickr for videos." Flickr was an existing photo-sharing site, then YouTube did a similar thing, except with videos.
- An online marketplace for college courses might be described as "Travelocity for online college classes."
- An online game rental service might be described as "Netflix for video games."
- A service that provides on-demand construction equipment might be described as "Uber for bulldozers"
- A quick-service Indian restaurant might be described as "Chipotle for curry"
- An executive coaching firm might be described as "Personal training for your business"

4. Solution

What is your solution (i.e., a product, a service, or combination) that solves your prospective customer's problems?

What are the features of your solution that solve the top problems of your customers? A feature is something that your solution does or has. Features can include how it looks, how it's bought, how it works, or how it meets a need.

5. Channels

What are ways that customers will find out about you?

6. Revenue Streams

What are the ways that you will make money?

What exactly will the customers pay you for?

What will the price be?

7. Cost structure

What costs would you incur just to get started? (fixed costs)

What costs would increase as you get more customers (variable costs)?

8. Key Metrics

What things will you measure to tell how your business is doing?

9. Unfair Advantage

What is something that your solution has that cannot be easily copied or bought by someone else?

Step 3. Describe your Minimum Viable Product (MVP)

Now review your Solution and envision the simplest (yet sellable) version of your Solution. It's called "minimum" since it should require the least amount of effort from you. It's called "viable" since it should be something that your Early Adopters will want to buy. Having an MVP allows you to test if your prospective customers are actually willing to buy from you, instead of just saying that they might buy from you.

- What could you offer for sale that would require the least amount of upfront work from you?
  - Describe this in a couple sentences or in enough detail that someone could decide if they are interested.
- Or even simpler, what could you sell before the product is ready to be delivered?

You may write your MVP at the bottom of the Lean Canvas page, or below.

My Minimum Viable Product:

_____

_____

_____

_____

Step 4. Write the script for the experiment

Next create a simple script that you could present to an Early Adopter to see if they want to buy. You can use this pattern:

Hi! My name is ***your name*** and I have noticed that ***description of your early adopters*** experience ***problems they face***. I am offering a description ***of your Minimum Viable Product*** at a price of _____. Would you be interested in buying that? If not, what would make my offer more interesting to you?

The next page has a fill-in-the blank version you can complete.

Sample script for presenting to an Early Adopter

Hi! My name is...

_____

(your name)

...and I have noticed that...

_____

_____

(describe the type of person or company that could be an early adopter of your MVP)

...experience...

_____

_____

(name a problem faced by your early adopters)

I am offering...

_____

_____

(give a brief description of your Minimum Viable Product)

...at a price of...

_____.

(list what you plan to charge for your MVP)

Would you be interested in buying that?

If not, what would make my offer more interesting to you?

Lean Canvas

PROBLEM	SOLUTION	UNIQUE VALUE PROPOSITION	UNFAIR ADVANTAGE	CUSTOMER SEGMENTS
	KEY METRICS	HIGH-LEVEL CONCEPT	CHANNELS	EARLY ADOPTERS
EXISTING ALTERNATIVES				

COST STRUCTURE	REVENUE STREAMS

CANVAS FILL ORDER

HIGH ITERATION PATH

CHAPTER 15
IMPROVE

Assembling a Toyota Prius at a manufacturing plant. A core principle of the Toyota Production System is kaizen, a Japanese word meaning "continuous improvement."

KEY QUESTION

How can I use an algorithm to improve something?

OBJECTIVES

After completing this chapter, students should be able to do the following:

1. Explain what the acronym DMAIC means.
2. Explain how DMAIC can be used to improve something.
3. Provide a few different examples of how DMAIC can be used.
4. Write a short summary of the chapter, answering the key question.

122

REVIEW QUESTIONS

Answer these questions with the help of the video:

1. What does the acronym DMAIC stand for?

_____

2. How can each letter in DMAIC help us to improve something?

_____

_____

_____

_____

3. What types of things could be improved in an oil refinery? in an ice cream shop?

_____

_____

_____

_____

4. What would be the first thing you would do to start the improvement process? What would you do as the second step?

_____

_____

_____

_____

_____

NOTES

_____

_____

_____

_____

_____

_____

_____

_____

_____

_____

_____

_____

_____

_____

DISCUSSION QUESTIONS

1. Instead of using the DMAIC process, what are less formal ways to improve something? When might those ways be appropriate?
2. What is the smallest amount of improvement that is worth doing? Why?
3. Are there times when we should not improve something? When and why?
4. How much time do you think it would take to make improvements in an oil refinery? Why?
5. How much time do you think it would take to make improvements in an ice cream shop? Why?
5. Some companies follow the Japanese practice of *kaizen*, which means "continuous improvement." What do you think that means, and how would a company or person implement that?

124

INVESTIGATION

In this Investigation you will explore **how to study for an upcoming math test** using an algorithmic, process-driven approach. We will apply a process called "DMAIC" (pronounced dee-may-ik) to think about how to improve your performance on the test. Each letter in DMAIC represents a different step in the improvement process.

For each step below, answer each of the questions in a complete sentence or with a complete list.

1. Define

What are all the topics that will be covered on the test? You may need to refer to your textbook, your syllabus, your notes, or you may need to ask your math teacher.

_____

_____

_____

How can you categorize the topics?

_____

_____

_____

What are all the types of questions that will be used on the test? For example, which of the following types of questions will appear: free response, multiple-choice, matching, essay, or other. You can refer to prior tests given by the same math teacher to see the types of questions that have been asked in the past.

_____

_____

_____

_____

_____

2. Measure

How can you assess your understanding of each topic and your ability to answer each type of question?

_____

_____

_____

What scoring system would be best to measure your performance in each area, before you take the actual test?

_____

_____

_____

3. Analyze

If your scoring system shows that you have not mastered a topic or type of question, what is the Root Cause of your underperformance?

_____

_____

_____

What concepts and skills do you need to acquire?

_____

_____

_____

What concepts and skills have the highest priority? Why?

_____

_____

_____

4. Improve
What are the solutions to the Root Cause(s) of your underperformance?

_____

_____

_____

List all the methods or techniques that you can use to address the Root Cause. Brainstorm as needed.

_____

_____

_____

5. Control
How will you be able to sustain the results you have achieved?

_____

_____

_____

What can you do just before the test to review?

_____

_____

_____

CHAPTER 16

CREATE

This score for the hymn "The western sky was purpled o'er" was handwritten by Charles Wesley (1707-1788) who composed over 6,000 hymns in his lifetime.

KEY QUESTION

How can I use an algorithm to create something?

OBJECTIVES

After completing this chapter, students should be able to do the following:
1. Explain how creative works can adhere to standards and constraints.
2. Provide examples of how artists, writers, and other creators can use algorithms and frameworks.
3. Explain how some types of poems are defined by their structure.
4. Write a short summary of the chapter, answering the key question.

REVIEW QUESTIONS

Answer these questions with the help of the video:

1. What are some similarities and differences between haikus, limericks, and sonnets?

_____

_____

_____

2. Write a haiku or limerick.

_____

_____

_____

_____

3. How are algorithms or formulas used in fictional stories, TV dramas, and nonfiction works?

_____

_____

_____

_____

_____

4. Why are frameworks useful for creating content?

_____

_____

_____

_____

NOTES

_____

_____

_____

_____

_____

_____

_____

_____

_____

_____

_____

_____

_____

_____

_____

_____

DISCUSSION QUESTIONS

1. Do you agree with the statement that "Creativity loves constraints?" Why or why not?
2. Do you prefer writing fiction or nonfiction? Why?
3. What types of algorithms could help with your writing?
4. How would a writing algorithm differ based on whether the work is fiction or nonfiction?
5. If you could write a book on any topic, what would it be? Why would you choose that topic?
6. What would be the first steps you would take to get started?

INVESTIGATION

In this Investigation you will explore how to create a nonfiction book using an algorithmic, process-driven approach. This Investigation allows us to "divide and conquer" to create something new and useful.

Your group will apply the step-by-step process shown below to co-author a book.

Note: this Investigation will cover Steps 1 through 4, below. We will also use the output of this Investigation for next chapter's "Collaborate" Investigation which will cover Steps 5 through 8.

How to Write a Book with Multiple Authors

1. **Define the overall topic** for the book.
You could also suggest the title of the book. This can be decided in a large group, or a small group, or by one person such as an instructor or group leader.

2. **Create chapter titles**
Brainstorm ideas and finalize the chapter topics and titles. You can use the "Brainstorm" Investigation to generate chapter ideas. Creating chapter titles can be done as a group (facilitated by the group leader) with each member of the group providing ideas. Or one group member can suggest a list of chapter topics.

3. **Assign chapters**
Assign one or more chapters to each person who will be doing the writing. Depending on your group size, you may need to assign more than one chapter to each person.

4. **Write the chapters**
Each author writes their assigned chapter(s).

5. **Edit the chapters**
Each team member edits a chapter that was written by someone else. You will do this as the next chapter Investigation, "Collaborate."

6. **Provide feedback** to the author.
You will provide ideas for improvement to the author.

7. **Respond to feedback** from your editor
Each team member answers questions and responds to feedback from their editor about the chapter.

8. **Combine the chapters** into a book
After the "Collaborate" Investigation is completed, all of the individual chapters will form a book. Congratulations! You have collaboratively written a book that covers your chosen topic!

Setting up this Investigation (for the instructor or group leader)
This Investigation requires a few items to be decided beforehand. These can be decided by the instructor or by each group that is collaborating to write a book.

a. Choose a book topic, so that every student can be assigned at least one chapter.
- Choose a book topic that is sufficiently complex or diverse, so that you will be able to create enough chapters. If there are more students than possible chapters, you can choose more than one book topic.
- Sample Book Topics
  - A Guide to different types of music
  - A Guide to helpful websites for _____
  - A Guide to the most popular _____
  - How to have a Great Summer Break
  - How to prepare for a ___ Test
  - A Guide to surviving __th Grade at our school
  - A Guide to being more active in our community
  - A Guide to eating healthier
  - A Guide to the leading cities and towns in our state
  - A Guide to restaurants in our city
  - A Guide to our city government (or state or county)

b. Create chapter titles
Each chapter title breaks down the Book Title into a component or particular aspect or subtopic.

c. Decide the target length of each chapter
This could be from 200 to 600 words, depending on the time available for this Investigation and the grade level of the students.

d. Decide how the written chapters will be shared with others. This will be important when we collaborate on the written material.
Possibilities include the following:
- Share online documents or folders (e.g., Google GSuite or Microsoft 365 or Dropbox)
- Share posts or documents in your Learning Management System
- Email the documents between the Author and Editor
- Share paper documents, if students are in the same location each day

e. Assign chapters to students. If you have more chapters than students, you can assign multiple chapters to one student.

Note: Give each student access to the document or folder they need to write their chapter.

134

Investigation Instructions for the student

1. Assemble the inputs you need for this Investigation, including the following:

- Your book's topic

  _____

- Your assigned chapter topic

  _____

  _____

- Any ideas related to your topic that you can brainstorm
  - If you need ideas, use a mindmap or brainstorming algorithm
- Your own experience and insights related to the topic.
- The document or folder where you will write your chapter

2. Use the template below (or one provided by your instructor) to outline a useful, readable chapter. Do not just type random ideas; you need to use a structure so that all the chapters will be consistent.

Sample chapter template

Introduction
        What is the chapter topic and how can you describe it in more detail?
        Why is this topic important, helpful, or useful?
        What will this chapter help people to do, related to this topic?
Key concepts
        What are new terms, ideas, or objectives related to this topic?
        What might someone need to know or do before fully understanding this topic?
Top Suggestions
        What are three to five top suggestions related to this topic?
        Do's and Don'ts:
                What should someone be sure to do related to this topic?
                What should someone be sure *not* to do related to this topic?
        What is a good process or sequence for someone to follow?
        What are instructions that will allow someone to make full use of these suggestions?
Challenges & Solutions
        What are some of the common obstacles, difficulties, or surprises that someone could face in this topic area?
        What are ways that someone could overcome these obstacles and difficulties?

3. Write a chapter about your assigned topic.
Make sure you reach the number of words that have been chosen as the target chapter length.
You will write a draft version of your chapter. This draft needs to be typewritten, not handwritten.

4. Place your draft chapter into the document or folder provided to you. This is the output of this Investigation.

CHAPTER 17
COLLABORATE

Four young men from Liverpool, England (John Lennon, Paul McCartney, George Harrison, and Richard Starkey) collaborated to write, perform, or record over 200 songs during the 1960's.

KEY QUESTION

How can I use an algorithm to collaborate with others?

OBJECTIVES

After completing this chapter, students should be able to do the following:

1. Name several different collaboration methods and the benefits of each.
2. Choose a collaboration method based on what is being created.
3. Write a short summary of the chapter, answering the key question.

REVIEW QUESTIONS

Answer these questions with the help of the video:

1. What is the difference between collaborating and communicating?

_____

_____

_____

2. What are some different patterns for collaborative authoring?

_____

_____

3. Which pattern seems most efficient or easiest? Which pattern seems least efficient? Why?

_____

_____

_____

_____

_____

_____

4. If you were collaborating with others to create something new, which method would you prefer? Why?

_____

_____

_____

_____

_____

_____

NOTES

_____

_____

_____

_____

_____

_____

_____

_____

_____

_____

_____

_____

_____

_____

_____

_____

DISCUSSION QUESTIONS

1. When have you needed to collaborate to accomplish something? What did you collaborate on? Did your collaboration process work well? If you could collaborate on that topic again, what would you do differently?

2. What skills does someone need to be an excellent collaborator? Why?

3. What occupations would require a lot of collaboration? For what purpose?

4. Would you enjoy working at that job? Why or why not?

INVESTIGATION

This Investigation will continue the collaboration algorithm that we are following to create a book. We will cover Step 5 (Edit the chapters), Step 6 (Provide feedback), and Step 7 (Respond to feedback).

You will collaborate with another student to refine what you wrote in the Chapter 16 Investigation.

You will assume two different Roles in this Investigation: Editor and Author.
- As Editor, you will be analyzing and improving a chapter that someone else has written.
- As Author, you will be responding to the feedback your Editor has provided.

Setting up this Investigation (for the instructor or group leader)
This Investigation requires a few items to be decided beforehand. These can be decided by the instructor or by the group, but make sure to write down the decisions.

a. Assign an editor to every chapter that has been written.
For example,
Chapter 1 was authored by _____ and will be edited by _____.
                                (person's name)   (a different person's name)
Chapter 2 was authored by _____ and will be edited by _____.
Chapter 3 was authored by _____ and will be edited by _____.
...and continue for all written chapters.

Tip: Publish the Editor assignments to a place where everyone can view them easily. This could be a Google Sheet, a page in your Learning Management System, an online document, a web page, or a blog post.

b. Decide how the text of each chapter can be easily shared between the Author and Editor. Possibilities include the following:
- Share an online document (e.g., Google GSuite or Microsoft 365 or Dropbox)
- Share a post or document in your Learning Management System
- Email the document between the Author and Editor
- Share paper documents, if students are in the same location each day

c. Create an "Editing Deadline"
This is when the Editor's changes and questions are due. Editors must finish editing all chapters assigned to them by this deadline.
        EDITING DEADLINE: _____
                        (date and time)

d. Create an "Author's Response Deadline"
This is when the Author's replies to the Editor's feedback is due. This should be at least one day after the Editing Deadline, so that the Author has time to read, evaluate, and respond to the Editor's feedback. Authors must respond to their Editor's comments and questions by this deadline.
        AUTHOR'S RESPONSE DEADLINE: _____
                              (date and time)

Investigation Instructions for the student

Now that the Investigation is set up, you can begin with Step 5, since this is where we left off in the prior Investigation.

Step 5. Edit the chapters
Note: Steps 5 and 6 must be completed by the Editing Deadline, listed above.

You will be assuming the role of Editor.
Access the person's chapter that you were assigned to edit, either online or on paper. Note this is different from the chapter you wrote.

Edit the chapter that you have been assigned, using the following checklist:
___ Format all of the text using 12-point normal text, Arial (or similar) font.

___ Arrange the text into sections, if the author has not already done this. Use a **14-point bold** font for each section heading. Possible section headings could include the following, but your results may vary:
- Introduction
- Key concepts
- Top Suggestions
- Challenges & Solutions

___ Include at least one sentence near the beginning of the chapter about why this chapter is relevant or useful.
___ Improve the grammar and style where needed. For example, change any sentences in the passive voice to active voice.
___ Fix any spelling errors that appear in the text.
___ Refine any passages or sentences that are unclear or too wordy. Try to retain all of the ideas and suggestions that the author makes. You can change the wording if it makes the chapter clearer, but don't remove any of the concepts.

Step 6. Provide improvement ideas for the author
___ Create a section at the bottom of the document and add the section heading "**Ideas for enhancing this chapter**"
Write down two ideas for making the chapter even better. These could be one of the following, or anything that could make the chapter better.
- A subtopic or point that you feel was omitted or covered too briefly.
- Something that needs more detail or explanation.
- An example that could be added.
- A long passage that could be divided into smaller sections to aid readability.

Note that the ideas you provide should be able to be implemented by the original author in 15 to 20 minutes total. So an idea like "rewrite this whole chapter" is not suitable for this Investigation.

If your idea relates to a specific passage or location in the chapter, you may use the highlighting or commenting feature in the software you are using.

___ Ask the author two questions.
Create a section at the bottom of the document and add the section heading **"Questions for the author"**
Write two (2) questions for the author to answer. These questions should be related to the chapter topic, and the spirit of the question should be to help the reader understand the topic better.

Step 7. Put on your "Author" hat and respond to the feedback from your Editor.
Note: This step must be completed after the Editing Deadline and before the Author's Response Deadline, listed above.
Go to the chapter that you originally authored (not the chapter you edited), and do the following:

___ Incorporate the ideas from Step 6 (above) into your chapter. This could involve answering a question or making changes to your original text.

___ Write complete answers to the two questions under "Questions for the author" that you were asked by your Editor.

Step 8. Combine the chapters into a book
Assign someone from your group to collect all the edited chapters into a single document. Then share that document with the group. Your book is ready to read!

REFERENCES

Chapter 1 Header Image
Poirer, Conrad. "Commercial. At the Coca Cola Plant." Wikimedia Commons, 2014,
commons.wikimedia.org.
Public Domain

Chapter 1, Investigation Scenario 1
Palmer, Mark. "Whole Foods from the Mezzanine." 2018
Used by permission

Chapter 1, Investigation Scenario 2
Hitchcock, Andrew, "Airplane Cockpit." Flickr.com, 2002.
Licensed under the Creative Commons Attribution 2.0 Generic license (CC BY 2.0)
https://creativecommons.org/licenses/by/2.0/legalcode

Chapter 1, Investigation Scenario 3
Galleri Beck-Fischer. "He Hongwei Artist Studio in Songzhuang." Flickr.com, 2010
Licensed under the Attribution-NoDerivs 2.0 Generic (CC BY-ND 2.0)
https://creativecommons.org/licenses/by-nd/2.0/legalcode

Chapter 1, Investigation Scenario 4
01-4-farm-iowa-1731523.jpg
Mark, David. "Iowa Farm: Silos, Barn, Wind Turbines" Pixabay.com, 2016
Licensed under the Pixabay license.
https://pixabay.com/service/terms/#license

Chapter 1, Investigation Scenario 5
Ogwen. "Atlantic - Pacific Shortcut: Container Ship leaving Miraflores Locks, Panama" Flickr.com, 2004
Licensed under the Creative Commons Attribution 2.0 Generic license (CC BY 2.0)
https://creativecommons.org/licenses/by/2.0/legalcode

Chapter 2, Header image
U.S. Bureau of Engraving and Printing, "Obverse of the series 2009 $100 Federal Reserve Note"
Wikimedia Commons, 2010, commons.wikimedia.org.
Public Domain

Chapter 3, Header image
National Hurricane Center, "Five-day forecast cone of uncertainty with track line for Matthew from the
National Hurricane Center, since 28 September 2016," Wikimedia Commons, 2016,
commons.wikimedia.com
Public Domain

Chapter 4, Header image
Govan, Donovan. "This is a sieve (also known as a strainer)." Wikimedia Commons, 2005,
commons.wikimedia.org.
Licensed under the Creative Commons Attribution-ShareAlike 3.0 Unported License (CC BY-SA 3.0)
https://creativecommons.org/licenses/by-sa/3.0/legalcode

Chapter 5, Header image
Niabot, "Menger Sponge after four iterations." Wikimedia Commons, 2005, commons.wikimedia.org.
Licensed under the Creative Commons Attribution-ShareAlike 3.0 Unported License (CC BY-SA 3.0)
https://creativecommons.org/licenses/by-sa/3.0/legalcode